Barcelona

Berlitz®
Barcelona

Text by Neil Schlecht
Revised by Pam Barrett
Photography by Neil Schlecht except
pages 27, 34, 37, 38, 60, 66, 87, 91 by
Bill Wassman/Apa, and pages 73, 75,
76, 93 by Claude Huber
Cover photograph by Neil Schlecht
Photo Editor: Naomi Zinn
Cartography by Raffaele De Gennaro

Tenth Edition 2002

CONTACTING THE EDITORS
Every effort has been made to provide accurate information in this publication, but
changes are inevitable. The publisher cannot be responsible for any resulting loss,
inconvenience or injury. We would appreciate it if readers would call our attention to
any errors or outdated information by contacting Berlitz Publishing, PO Box 7910,
London SE1 1WE, England. Fax: (44) 20 7403 0290;
e-mail: berlitz@apaguide.demon.co.uk

*Printed in Singapore by Insight Print Services (Pte) Ltd, 38 Joo Koon Road, Singapore
628990. Tel: (65) 6865-1600. Fax: (65) 6861-6438*

*Berlitz Trademark Reg. U.S. Patent Office and other countries. Marca Registrada.
Used under licence from the Berlitz Investment Corporation*

040/210 REV

CONTENTS

Barcelona and the Catalans	7
A Brief History	13
Where to Go	23
La Rambla	23
Barri Gòtic	30
La Ribera	40
El Eixample & Modernisme	46
La Sagrada Família	56
Waterfront and Barceloneta	59
El Raval	64
Montjuïc	67
The Diagonal	71
Tibidabo	72
Excursions	74

What to Do 81

Shopping 81
Entertainment 87
Sports 91
Barcelona for Children 93

Eating Out 95

Handy Travel Tips 102

Hotels and Restaurants 128

Index 143

● A  in the text denotes a highly recommended sight

Barcelona

BARCELONA AND THE CATALANS

Barcelona may be the second city of Spain, locked in eternal rivalry with Madrid, but it ruled an empire long before Spain was even born. Some 2,000 years ago, the Romans, on their way to conquering the whole of Iberia, built a forbidding wall around their settlement on the Mediterranean coast and called it *Barcino*.

Today, a visitor could spend days wandering the Gothic Quarter, an atmospheric tangle of medieval buildings and alleyways where the city's glorious past is palpable, but Barcelona is anything but a musty old history lesson. It is a dynamic, densely populated, and daringly modern metropolis. Since hosting the 1992 Olympic Games, the city, capital of the autonomous region of Catalonia, has in many ways eclipsed Madrid and become one of Europe's hottest cities.

Spain's mid-1980s induction into the European Union and Barcelona's triumphant 1992 Olympic experience have rejuvenated the city. Once grimy and grey, with a smelly industrial port that pushed this former maritime power away from the sea, Barcelona has reinvented itself. Badly needed new circulation routes were built, rundown neighbourhoods have been reborn and numerous "urban spaces", featuring sculpture and greenery, have been created. Throughout the late 1980s and the 1990s, the city, with characteristic energy, underwent a massive facelift. The airport and railway stations (particularly the Estació de França) were brought up to date, and new museums, concert halls, and hotels sprang up.

The most important physical change, though, has been Barcelona's reorientation towards the sea: The city now embraces the Mediterranean. With its newly dynamic port that is now one of the busiest cruise-ship stops in Europe, its clean urban beaches, and renowned seafront neighbourhoods, the Catalan capital has succeeded in marrying the seductive pleasures of the Mediterranean with the sophisticated, creative energy of modern Europe.

Barcelona's physical transformation has accompanied a rebirth of Catalan culture, long marginalised – often overtly repressed – by Spanish rulers. The most ruthless aggression came during the Franco dictatorship, lasting from the 1936–39 Spanish Civil War, during which Barcelona was a Republican stronghold, till the dictator's death in 1975. Under the Statue of Autonomy in 1978, Catalonia regained a large substantial measure of self government, and today Catalan arts and literature, as well as the native tongue, are vigorously promoted by the Catalan government.

Reawakened, too, is the pride Barceloneses take in their city. They are proud of their architecture and design. The man behind much of it is the city's most famous son, Antoni Gaudí (1852–1926), eccentric architect and one of the foremost creators of *modernisme,* Catalan Art Nouveau. Gaudí's buildings still startle: his soaring, unfinished cathedral, La Sagrada Família, whose spires drip like melting candles, is his best-known work, but there are scores more in Barcelona. Buildings moulded like ocean waves, roofs shaped like dragon scales, chimneys straight out of *Star Wars.* And that's just Gaudí; around the turn of the century, a group of *modernistas*, including Lluís Domènech i Montaner and Josep Puig i Cadafalch, dreamed up the most fanciful buildings their rich imaginations and equally rich patrons would allow.

Barcelona also nurtured the careers of some of the 20th-century's greatest artists – native sons Joan Miró and Salvador Dalí, and Pablo Picasso, who spent his formative years in the Catalan capital before seeking fame in Paris (Barcelona's Picasso museum has the largest collection of his work outside Paris). Few other cities are as design-mad as Barcelona. The opening of every high-tech museum, bridge, and bar is a public event discussed and debated by local people. Thirty thousand people visited Richard Meier's Museum of Contemporary Art (MACBA) on its first weekend, though there was scarcely a work of art in the place. Couples rush to place their wedding registers at the trendiest design shops, and avant-garde public spaces are analysed thoughtfully and, more often than not, publicly funded.

In a city with such a wild streak, Barceloneses tend to be surprisingly conservative and very pragmatic. Spain's industrial juggernaut, Barcelona is dead serious about work and money. With 15 percent of Spain's population (1.6 million in the city itself), Catalonia produces more than 20 percent of the country's GDP and a quarter of all exports. Catalans have a reputation for being tight with money – a criticism that's mostly a backhanded compliment acknowledging that they certainly know how to earn and manage it.

The city's seriousness of purpose extends to its history and culture. Rituals like the *sardana,* a traditional dance performed every Sunday morning in front of the cathedral, are held almost sacred. Men, women, and children

Portrait painters ply their trade on Las Ramblas.

A swing bridge leads to the attractions on the Moll d'Espanya in Port Vell.

hold hands and form a circle – women pragmatically placing their bags in the centre – and perform the apparently simple but very regimented steps. They gather on saints' days and regional holidays to cheer on *castellers*, human towers of men and boys forming up to seven levels of bodies stretching towards the sky. Catalans have held onto their language tenaciously, defending it against repeated attempts from Castile, and the Franco government, to extinguish it. Above all, in their minds the Catalan homeland is a *pays* – a country, not a mere region.

Barcelona has long been considered different from the rest of Spain, and though visitors can attend a bullfight or flamenco show, this really isn't the place for such typically Spanish practices. The city is famous for its stubborn sense of independence and identity – and how "un-Spanish" it feels. You'll see T-shirts proclaiming that "Catalunya is not Spain", and hear shopkeepers responding to Spanish speakers in Catalan – bilingual conversations that can be harmless or political, depending upon the participants. While there are many who would prefer Barcelona to be the capital of an independent, Catalan-speaking nation, most of these hard-working people are simply frustrated that so much local wealth is rerouted to Madrid.

All political considerations are cast aside, though, when seemingly the whole of Barcelona takes to the streets just before lunch or in the early evening. *Las Ramblas*, a tree-lined boulevard Victor Hugo called "the most beautiful in the world", is packed with local people and tourists, both groups equally delighted to be there. Boisterous patrons spill out of corner bars, where they've dipped in to eat *tapas* (an array of snacks that might include a wedge of omelet, sardines, octopus, olives, cheese, *chorizo* sausage, and much more) and have a glass of wine, beer, or local *cava* (sparkling wine that comes from just outside Barcelona). Mimes strike poses for photos and spare change, and older people take a seat to watch the whole parade stream by.

Take your cue from local people and La Rambla: Barcelona is an ideal city for walking. Hemmed in by the sea and hills on three sides, the city is surprisingly manageable. It spills down a gentle slope to the waterfront. Near the water is the Barri Gòtic (Gothic Quarter) and the rest of the old city, a labyrinth of streets inhabited for a thousand years. Ancient stones of the Roman city are visible in columns and walls, and in underground passages – the settlement's original foundations – you can visit beneath the *Museu d'Història de la Ciutat*. Barcelona grew out of its original walls, and its modern sectors extend northeast, away from the sea. There are only a handful of highrise buildings, and the avenues are broad and leafy, punctuated by squares crowded with cafés. The Eixample district, a grid of streets laid out in the 19th century, includes landmark *modernista* apartment buildings, fashionable boutiques, galleries, restaurants, and hotels.

Barcelona is every bit as spirited at night as it is during the day. Residents begin their evenings with *tapas* and rounds of drinks after work, activities that put dinner off until a fashionably – some might say absurdly – late hour. Ten o'clock is normal but it's not uncommon for Barceloneses to sit down to dinner in a restaurant once the clock has already struck midnight. If it's a real night out, it's on from there to bars, live-music venues, and discos, many of which don't really get going until 2 or 3am. If you're up at daybreak on a Friday, Saturday, or Sunday, you'll see plenty of bleary-eyed locals straggling home. Any day of the week, the Ramblas pulsates with life, in all its manifestations, into the wee hours. If late-night Barcelona is too wild for your tastes, an evening stroll before or after dinner is also a highlight: the cathedral and other churches, palaces, and monuments, including several principal *modernista* buildings, are illuminated. The *Barri Gòtic* retreats to a medieval silence, broken only by the sharp sounds of a family quarrel in close-knit quarters or the animated hollering of late-night revellers prowling the bars.

As Robert Hughes points out in his book *Barcelona*, the name of the largest hill overlooking the city, Tibidabo, is Latin for "I will give you" – the words the devil spoke to

Jesus, looking down from high on a mountain as he tempted him with earthly delights. You'll be similarly tempted – by the city's revolutionary architecture and design, its splendid Gothic quarter, the lively Ramblas and waterfront, the cafés, bars, restaurants, and the nightlife. Accept the offer.

Barcelona's beaches can get crowded at times.

A BRIEF HISTORY

Barcelona was originally called Barcino, named for the Carthaginian general and father of Hannibal, Hamilcar Barca, who established a base on the northeastern coast of Iberia in 237 BC. Phoenicians and Greeks had previously settled the area, and Barcino occupied the site of an earlier Celtiberian settlement called Laie. But the Romans, who conquered all of Iberia, left the most indelible marks on Barcelona. They defeated the Carthaginians in 206 BC. and ruled Spain for the next 600 years, a period in which Roman law, language, and culture took firm root across the peninsula. The Roman citadel in Barcelona, surrounded by a massive wall, occupied high ground where the cathedral and city hall now stand. From the 1st century AD, Christian communities spread through Catalonia.

After sacking Rome in AD 410, the Visigoths swept into Spain. They adopted Barcelona as their capital from 531 until 554, when they moved it to Toledo. The invasion of the Moors in 713 brought the Visigothic kingdom to an end, and Catalonia was briefly overrun by the invaders from Africa. After their defeat beyond the Pyrenees by the Franks in 801, the Moors withdrew, and retained no lasting foothold in Catalonia, which is why there is little visible Moorish influence there today. Charlemagne's knights installed themselves in the border counties to guard the southern flank of his empire.

A feudal lord, Guifré el Pélos – Wilfred the Hairy – became the Count of Barcelona. In 878 he founded a dynasty that would rule for nearly five centuries. While much of Spain was under Moorish domination, Barcelona and most of Catalonia remained linked to northern Europe, a geopolitical wrinkle that would do much to determine the distinct Catalan character.

The neo-Gothic church of Sagrat Cor on Tibidabo.

Catalonia's legendary founding father also gave the budding nation its flag of four horizontal red stripes on a gold field, the oldest still in use in Europe. Legend holds that the stripes were etched in Wilfred's blood, drawn on his shield as an escutcheon by the fingers of the Frankish king after the count had courageously defended his overlord in a battle.

When King Louis V refused to come to their aid against Moorish raiders, the counts of Barcelona declared their independence in 988, a date celebrated as Catalonia's birth as a nation-state. The Catalan nation was soon enlarged through marriage and military adventure. Ramón Berenguer III (1096–1131) captured Mallorca, Ibiza, and Tarragona from the Moors and acquired the French county of Provence through his wife. His successor, Ramón Berenguer IV, united Catalonia with neighbouring Aragón by marriage, and his son, Alfonso II, became the first joint king of Aragón and Catalonia and was known as "the Emperor of the Pyrenees". His kingdom extended all the way to Nice.

But much of this territory was lost by the next king, Alfonso's son Peter (Pere) the Catholic, who picked the losing side in the French crusade against the heretics of Albi.

Successive generations turned their attention towards the conquest of the Mediterranean basin. Jaume I (1213–76), known as "the Conqueror", consolidated control over the Balearic Islands and claimed Valencia. Sicily was annexed in 1282 and over the ensuing century, Barcelona reached the peak of its glory. Its mercantilist trade grew rapidly throughout the Mediterranean, and its territories included Sardinia, Corsica, Naples and the Roussillon in southern France.

The Middle Ages, from the late 13th–15th centuries, were a time of great building in Barcelona, giving rise to the cathedral and other great Gothic palaces and monuments. Wedged between Europe and the Muslim territories, Barcelona served as a channel for the exchange of scientific knowledge and scholarship. The arts flourished in the cities and monasteries of Catalonia, patronised by a vigorous class of artisans, bankers, and merchants, including an important Jewish community.

Nascent political institutions had appeared, with a code of laws, the *Usatges de Barcelona*, in the 11th century; a municipal council with participation of leading citizens called the *Consell de Cent* (Council of One Hundred) in 1249; and in 1359 the Corts Catalanes, or Catalan parliament, which had been meeting irregularly since the 1280s, was officially appointed. A body which later become the *Generalitat*, was set up to regulate financial and political concerns.

Barcelona's fate took another decisive turn when the marriage of Ferdinand of Aragón-Catalonia (Ferrán II to the Catalans) to Isabella of Castile joined their two crowns and formed the nucleus of a united Spanish state. Under the *Reyes Católicos* – the Catholic Monarchs, so-called because they captured Granada, the last Moorish redoubt on the peninsula, in 1492 – Catalonia was fully incorporated into Castile. After Christopher Columbus's voyage to the Americas, he was received by the monarchs in Barcelona's Royal Palace. Despite the symbolic gesture, Castile, the power centre of Spain, exclusively exploited New World riches, excluding

Barcelona for 300 years. The Catholic church's hard-line Inquisition expelled Jews from Spain and communities in Barcelona and Girona were particularly affected.

During the 16th century, a Golden Age for Spain, the political influence of Catalonia and Barcelona declined even further. The Habsburg grandson of Ferdinand and Isabella was anointed Charles I of Spain in 1516. He inherited the title of Holy Roman Emperor and became Charles V, with duties throughout Europe that gave him little time for Spain. His son Philip II moved the capital of the great Spanish empire from Toledo to previously insignificant Madrid.

In 1640, with Spain and France involved in the Thirty Years' War, Catalonia declared itself an independent republic, allied to Philip IV's enemy, France. After the French defeat in 1659, the Catalan territories north of the Pyrenees were ceded to France, fixing the border where it is today. The ensuing years were rife with wars, shifting alliances and disputes over succession to the crown. In all these conflicts, Barcelona automatically sided with whoever opposed Madrid, and usually ended up the loser.

The worst of these episodes came in the War of the Spanish Succession (1701–13) between the backers of Philip of Anjou, the 17-year-old grandson of Louis XIV of France, and the Habsburg claimant, Archduke Charles of Austria. Charles was enthusiastically received when he landed in Catalonia, but Philip, supported by France, won the war and became the first Bourbon ruler as Philip V. After a 13-month siege, on 11 September 1714, the royal army captured and sacked Barcelona. The Catalan Generalitat was dissolved and the city's privileges were abolished. The Ciutadella fortress was built to keep the populace subdued, and official use of the Catalan language was outlawed. Catalonia celebrates this defeat as its national holiday, a symbol of the spirit of nationalist resistance.

Discord within the Spanish government or conflict with foreign powers frequently served as an excuse for Catalan separatists to rise up, though their rebellions were usually summarily quashed. From 1808 to 1814, Spain again became a battleground, with British forces taking on Napoleon's troops in the Peninsular War. Napoleon attacked and destroyed Catalonia's sacred shrine, the monastery at Montserrat.

The spirit of European liberalism was late in reaching Spain. After many reverses, a republic, a constitutional monarchy and a democratic constitution were instituted in 1873. Shortly afterwards, Barcelona was at long last given the right to trade with the colonies of the New World.

Meanwhile, the city had gone about its business, devoting its energies to industrialisation. Barcelona's medieval walls were torn down to make way for an expansion in the mid-19th century. The Eixample, an elegant modern district, was laid out on a grid of broad avenues where the new industrialists built

Modern apartments and contemporary sculpture.

mansions. Wealthy patrons supported such architects as Antoni Gaudí and Lluís Domènech i Muntaner, who embraced *modernisme*. Prosperity was accompanied by a revival in Catalan arts and letters, a period known in Catalan as the *Renaixença* (Renaissance). In a burst of optimism, the city bid for world-wide recognition with the Universal Exposition of 1888, built on the site of the Ciutadella fortress.

With the industrial expansion, an urban working class evolved in Barcelona. Agitation for social justice and region-alist ferment created a combustible atmosphere, and the city became the scene of strikes and anarchist violence. The mod-ern Socialist Party and the UGT, Spain's largest trade union, were both founded at this time. For their part, industrialists sought Catalan autonomy as a way to be freed from interfer-ence (and taxation) from Madrid. In 1914 a provincial gov-ernment, the *Mancomunitat*, was formed, uniting the four Catalan provinces – Barcelona, Tarragona, Lérida, and Gerona – was formed. The region profited from Spanish neu-trality in World War I, by trading with both sides.

The *Mancomunitat* was dissolved in 1924 by General Primo de Rivera, who established a military dictatorship and banned the Catalan language. Despite this, Barcelona plunged energetically into preparations for another International Exhibition, with monumental buildings, pavilions, and sports facilities erected on Montjuïc hill. It opened a few months before the stock market crash of 1929.

In 1931, the Second Republic was established, and King Alfonso XIII escaped to exile. Catalonia won a charter es-tablishing home rule, restoration of the regional parliament and flag, and recognition of Catalan as the official language of the region. For the next several years the pendulum of power in Spain swung back and forth. The army rebelled in 1936, ini-tiating the brutal and bloody Civil War. Many churches in

The Catalan Tongue

Street signs and menus – and the unfamiliar words emanating from the local people – are enough to reveal that Barcelona differs from the rest of Spain. Those words with all the *xs* and *nys*, and idiosyncracies like double consonants divided by a full stop, as in paral.lel, are Catalan, the language – and national pride of the people. Catalan is not a dialect of Castilian Spanish, but an independent, ancient language. Long repressed and stigmatised, Catalan is once again a living language in Catalonia.

Catalan developed from spoken Latin during the Roman rule of Iberia. The language is closest to *Provençal*, the defunct tongue of southern France. Outside Catalonia, Catalan is spoken in Valencia, Alicante, the Balearic Islands, the principality of Andorra (where it is the official language), and north of the French border as far as Perpignan– some seven million people in all speak Catalan. There is a rich literature in the language, dating from the 9th century to the present.

In the 18th century, Philip V tried to abolish the language, to punish the region for supporting a rival to his throne. General Franco's suppression of Catalan after the Civil War in 1939 drove it underground and made it a rallying point for political opposition. Under the Constitution of 1978, Catalan became the mother tongue of Catalonia, the official language of the Autonomous Region, and along with Castilian, an official language of Spain.

Both Catalan and Castilian are required for graduation from all schools. Most public education is in Catalan, but there are schools where Castilian is the first language of instruction. Fluent Catalan is required for most government jobs. Barcelona natives are split between those who speak Catalan (and prefer not to speak anything else) and those who don't – incomers from other parts of Spain who have not learned it. Visitors who understand French and Spanish can usually understand some Catalan.

19

Barcelona were put to the torch by anti-clerical mobs. The city, firmly Republican, briefly became the capital in late 1937 and was a rallying point for the International Brigade. Barcelona was one of the last cities to fall to the rebel troops of General Francisco Franco at the war's end in 1939.

The Civil War ended with some 700,000 combatants dead on both sides; another 30,000 were executed or assassinated, including many priests and nuns; perhaps as many as 15,000 civilians were killed in air raids and numerous refugees left the country. Barcelona was repeatedly bombed, and its people suffered great hardship. Much bitterness had been sown.

One of the extraordinary modernista buildings to be seen in Barcelona.

Catalonia paid a heavy price in defeat. Franco abolished all regional institutions and established central government controls. The Catalan language was again proscribed, even in schools and churches. For years, Barcelona received little financial support from Madrid, and Spain remained essentially cut off from the rest of Europe.

Nevertheless, the city's industry recovered; people in search of work flocked to the Barcelona area from less prosperous parts of Spain, and huge, barren dormitory suburbs were constructed to house them. From the 1960s a tourism boom along the Costa Brava helped the local economy and brought the people of Franco's conservative Spain in touch with modern Europe.

When Franco died in 1975, Spain rapidly emerged from its isolation. The coronation of his designated successor, Juan Carlos, the grandson of Alfonso XIII, brought the restoration of parliamentary democracy and a relaxation of some rigid laws. The 1978 Constitution granted degrees of autonomy to Spain's fractious regions. While a militant Basque minority demanded greater independence and resorted to terrorist tactics that continue to this day, most Catalans were content with the restoration of the Generalitat and the return of Catalan as an official language, although there are some who call for total independence. Pasqual Maragall, a socialist, became mayor of Barcelona and a year later Jordi Pujol, leader of the conservative Convergència party, became president of Catalonia.

Felipe González, a charismatic socialist, was prime minister of Spain from 1982 to 1986 and Spain became a member of the European Economic Community (now European Union, or EU) in 1986, hastening the country's modernisation. The EU's freeing of trade tariffs and controls, and Barcelona's hosting of the 1992 Olympic Games, acted as catalysts for the city and Catalonia to embark on a significant economic boom. A radical urban policy brought about a huge wave of building activity in Barcelona, which furthered the transformation of the city.

In 1996, the surging Partido Popular, led by a rather uncharismatic former accountant, José María Aznar, was elected, forming the first conservative government in Spain since the return of democracy. In Barcelona, Maragall stepped down in 1997 and was succeeded by his deputy, Joan Clos. Two years later Maragall ran for leadership of the Catalan Generalitat but was defeated by Pujol.

Historical Landmarks

237 BC Carthaginian Hamilcar Barca makes base at Barcino.

206 BC Romans defeat Carthaginians.

531–54 Barcelona capital of Visigoths.

711 Moorish invasion of Spain. They remain there till 1492.

878 Wilfred the Hairy founds dynasty of counts of Barcelona.

1096–1131 Ramón Berenguer III extends Catalan empire.

1213–76 Jaume I consolidates empire, expands Barcelona.

1359 Corts (Parliament) of Catalonia established.

1469 Ferdinand and Isabella unite Aragón and Castile.

1494 Administration of Catalonia put under Castilian control.

1516 Charles I (Charles V, Holy Roman Emperor) takes throne.

1639 Catalonia sides with France in the Thirty Year' War.

1659 Catalan territories north of Pyrenees ceded to France.

1701–13 War of Spanish Succession.

1713–14 Siege of Barcelona by Philip V; Ciutadella fortress built.

1808–14 Peninsular War between England and France.

1888 Barcelona hosts its first Universal Exposition.

1914 Mancomunitat formed in Catalonia.

1923 General Primo de Rivera sets up military dictatorship, bans Catalan language and dissolves Mancomunitat.

1931 Republican party comes to power.

1932 Catalonia wins home rule.

1936–39 Civil War ends in Franco's rule, isolates Spain.

1975 Franco dies, Juan Carlos becomes king.

1978 Statue of Autonomy, Catalan language restored.

1986 Spain joins European Community (now European Union).

1992 The Olympics are held in Barcelona.

1997 Joan Clos becomes mayor of Barcelona.

2002 Barcelona works towards its target, the Universal Forum of Cultures (Barcelona 2004).

WHERE TO GO

Barcelona can be approached by neighbourhood or by theme. You can set out to see the Gothic Quarter, Montjuïc hill, or the waterfront; or you can create a greatest-hits tour of Gaudí and his fellow *Modernista* architects. It's tempting to try to sandwich everything into a couple of days, but leave time in your schedule to get sidetracked in a colourful food market or an alley of antiques shops, or to peek in a quiet courtyard. Take a breather, sinking into a chair at a pavement café to linger over a drink and snack, read a newspaper, and people-watch.

In the old town, where many streets are too narrow for cars and a slow pace is rewarded with the discovery of hidden treasures, the best way to travel is on foot. Each district of the old quarter – Barri Gòtic, La Ribera, El Raval, Las Ramblas – and the Eixample district can be covered as a walking tour. For sights farther afield, including Montjuïc, Barceloneta and the waterfront, Tibidabo, and two of the top Gaudí attractions, La Sagrada Família and Parque Güell, it's best to make use of Barcelona's excellent public transportation network – clean and efficient metro trains, modern buses, funiculars, and cable cars – as well as plenty of inexpensive taxis *(see Public Transport, p. 121)*. A good map is essential, but it's easy to be fooled by how close things look on paper.

LA RAMBLA

To call La Rambla a street is to do it woeful injustice. Barcelona's most famous boulevard–energetic, artistic, democratic, and indulgent–is an intoxicating parade of humanity. You'll no doubt want to sample it several times during your stay (maybe even several times a day). It is most crowded just before the (late) lunch hour and in the early

The medieval district, Barri Gòtic, offers a view into the long, rich history of the city.

evening on weekdays and at dusk at weekends, though it is never deserted. In the wee hours it's populated by a sometimes motley mix of early-morning newspaper sellers, street-sweepers, and bar hounds stumbling back to their apartments and hotels.

The broad, tree-shaded, promenade stretches nearly 2 km (1 mile) down a gentle incline from the city's hub, Plaça de Catalunya *(see page 54)*, to the waterfront. La Rambla takes its name from an Arabic word meaning a sandy, dry river bed. It was a shallow gully until the 14th century, when Barcelona families began to construct homes nearby. As the area became more populated, the stream was soon paved over. To the north of La Rambla (left as you walk down it) is the old city, Ciutat Vella; to the south, or right, is El Raval.

The five sections of La Rambla change in character, as they do in name, as you stroll along. The short **Rambla de Canaletes** at the top, named after the Font de Canaletes, the fountain that is one of the symbols of the city, is where crowds pour in from the Plaça de Catalunya or emerge from the metro and railway stations beneath. On Sunday and Monday in season you'll find rambunctious knots of fans replaying the games of Barça, Barcelona's beloved football club Barcelona FC; if an important match has just been won, look out. Here, too, begin the stalls where you can buy a diverse selection of foreign newspapers and magazines, as well as books, a reflection of Barcelona's status as Spain's publishing centre. You'll also see the first of the popular "human statues", portraying Christopher Columbus, a priest, a bearded nun, or a Roman soldier, among many guises.

Next up is **Rambla dels Estudis** popularly called Rambla dels Ocells (Rambla of the Birds) because here the boulevard narrows to become an outdoor aviary where winged creatures of all descriptions are sold. When the vendors leave at the end of the day, their cage-lined stalls are folded and shut like wardrobes, with the birds rustling about inside. Birds give way to flowers in the **Rambla de les Flors,** officially the Rambla de Sant Josep. People flock here on 23 April, the feast day of Sant Jordi (St George), celebrated as Day of the Book (because it is also the anniversary of Cervantes' death). A woman traditionally gives her man a book, and a man gives a women a rose—both of which are available in abundance along La Rambla. Keep an eye peeled on the right side of the road for the delectable *modernista* pastry shop, **Escribà** (Antiga Casa Figueres), its fanciful swirls on the outside a match for the delicacies within.

Facing the Rambla is the elegant **Palau de la Virreina,** a palace completed in 1778 for the young widow of the viceroy of colonial Peru. At street level is a branch of the city's Department of Culture where tickets to cultural events are

---

Más Ramblas

La Rambla is officially called Las Ramblas, as it comprises five sections, all with distinct formal and informal names. They meld so easily together that most Barceloneses call the whole affair by the singular, La Rambla.

sold, and information about museums and current exhibitions is available. The palace houses a museum with rotating contemporary art exhibits.

On the right-hand side of the street is one of La Rambla's great attractions and a constant in the life of Barceloneses: the Mercat de Sant Josep, usually called **La Boqueria**. This ornate, 19th-century covered market is an overflowing cornucopia of delights for the senses: fresh fish, meats, sausages, fruits and vegetables, and all kinds of spices, neatly braided ropes of garlic, sun-dried tomatoes and peppers, preserves, and sweetmeats, to make a gourmand swoon. La Boqueria is also a startlingly vibrant community, where shoppers and merchants greet each other by name, ribald sallies across the aisles set off gales of laughter, and the freshness of the *rape* (an angler fish popular in Catalonia) is debated with passion. The huge market is laid out under high-ceilinged ironwork naves, like a railway station. Restaurants in and near the market are like first-aid stations for those who become faint with hunger at the sight of such bounty. The market opens before dawn and keeps going till early evening. The best time to visit is when practised shoppers and restaurateurs go: early in the morning.

> It is said that if you drink from the Font de Canaletes you will return to Barcelona.

The heart of the Ramblas is nearby, at the **Pla de la Boqueria**, a busy intersection near the Liceu metro station paved with an unmistakable Joan Miró mosaic. Here stands one of Europe's great opera houses, the **Gran Teatre del Liceu**, inaugurated in 1861. Montserrat Caballé and Josep Carreras made their reputations singing here, a monument of the Catalan Renaissance and refuge of the Catalan elite. The opera house was gutted by a terrible fire in 1994 (the third it has suffered), forcing its closure. After a stunning restoration project that preserved the soul of the historic theatre while adding technological improvements and doubling the overall size to equip this magnificent opera house for the 21st century, the Liceu re-opened in 1999.

Directly across the Rambla is the venerable **Café de l'Opera**, a handsome, old-world café that's always bursting with patrons. It's a good spot for refreshment before you push on down the next stretch, the **Rambla dels Caputxins**. The Rambla's demeanour, like the incline, proceeds downhill after the Liceu, but the street-entertainment factor rises in inverse proportion. You'll wade your way through jugglers, human statues, fire-eaters, tarot-card readers, lottery-ticket sellers, mendicants, and many artists rapidly knocking out portraits, caricatures, and chalk master-work reproductions on the pavement.

On the right side of the street is the **Hotel Oriente**, which preserves a 17th-century Franciscan convent and cloister inside. Note the naïve painted angels floating over the doorway at Ernest Hemingway's favourite Barcelona lodging. Just beyond the hotel on the Carrer Nou de la Rambla is **Palau Güell,** the mansion Gaudí *(see page 50)* built in 1885 for his principal patron, textile tycoon Count Eusebi Güell. This

"Human statues" are a tourist attraction on La Rambla.

The Rambla de les Flores is fragrant with the scent of flowers that are sold on its stalls all year round.

meticulously detailed, fortress-like building, a study in high Gothic mingled with the architect's unmistakable touches, is open for guided tours. Visitors get to see the fabulously tiled rooftop chimneys, which were hidden from view for decades.

Returning to the Rambla, cross over and take the short stretch that leads into the arcaded **Plaça Reial.** This handsome, spacious square is graced with a fountain, palm trees, and wrought-iron lamp-posts designed by the young Gaudí. Like the Boqueria, the Hotel Oriente, and other Rambla landmarks, this square came into being as a result of the destruction of a convent, when church properties were expropriated in an anti-clerical period in the mid-19th century. Despite efforts to clean it up, it is still the stomping grounds of junkies and petty thieves, and there is always a police presence, but it is flush with bars, cafés, restaurants, a jazz club and a flamenco bar, and buzzing with action night and day.

The final promenade leading down to the harbour is the short **Rambla de Santa Mònica**, beginning at the Plaça del Teatre, site of the run-down **Teatre Principal**. The **Centre d'Art Santa Mònica**, in a converted convent, puts on fine contemporary art exhibits. The warren of alleys to the right is the once-notorious Barri Xino, or Chinatown, and still pretty seedy. It's not the best place for a midnight stroll but some of the old bars are becoming fashionable again and the atmospheric Pastís bar hasn't changed in decades.

Carrer dels Escudellers, a busy pedestrian street on the other side of the Rambla, is the gateway to a district of cabarets, bars, flamenco shows, and restaurants, and the delights of the Gothic Quarter. At its far end, the newly-created Plaça George Orwell is becoming trendy. Nearer the port is the **Museu de Cera** (Wax Museum), a tourist trap with more 300 realistic wax effigies. The Rambla ends at the broad, open space facing the **Monument a Colom,** a statue honouring the discoverer Christopher Columbus (*Colom* in Catalan) that can be climbed for good views of the port. He is supposed to be indicating the way to the New World, but he's actually pointing at Mallorca or perhaps North Africa. Just beyond the statue is Barcelona's newly revitalised waterfront.

Exotic chimneys were a feature of Gaudí's architectural style.

BARRI GÒTIC

From its beginnings more than 2,000 years ago, Barcelona has grown outwards in rings, like concentric ripples on a pond. The ancient core is a hill the Romans called Mont Tàber, where they raised a temple to Augustus Caesar and in the 4th century AD. built high walls about 1/2 km (1 mile) around to protect their settlement. This is the nucleus of the medieval district called the Barri Gòtic. While much of it is not technically Gothic, it is a remarkable concentration of medieval palaces, convents, and churches.

The best place to begin a tour is the superb **Catedral**, which is the neighbourhood's major site and focal point. The cathedral was begun in 1298 on the site of earlier churches going back to Visigothic times. The final touch – the rather florid Gothic façade – was not completed until the end of the 19th century and thus contrasts with the simple octagonal towers. The ribs of the cathedral's high vault are joined at carved and painted keystone medallions, a typically Catalan feature. In the centre of the nave is a splendid Gothic choir with lacy spires of carved wood. Above these are the heraldic emblems of the European kings and princes invited by Charles V to be members of his exclusive Order of the Golden Fleece *(Toison d'Or)*.

The Cathedral is even more impressive when illuminated against the night sky.

The first and only meeting was held in the cathedral in 1519. The seats reserved for Henry VIII of England and François I of France are next to the emperor's, but they didn't turn up.

Connected to the choir is a pulpit with an exceptional wrought-iron stair rail. Ahead, steps under the altar lead to the alabaster tomb of Santa Eulàlia, one of the city's two patron saints, martyred in the fourth century. On the wall of the right aisle are the tombs of Count Ramón Berenguer I and his wife Almodis, who founded the earlier cathedral on this spot in 1058. Don't

> For the opening times and phone numbers of most of the major museums and galleries, see pages 79–80. There is an entry fee unless stated otherwise. For other museums, remember that most close on Monday, and many for an hour or two at lunchtime. Churches are usually open all day.

miss the Catalan Gothic altarpieces in the chapels behind the altar; the nine panels of the Transfiguration painted for the Sant Salvador chapel in the 15th century by Bernat Martorell are considered his masterpiece.

The leafy **cloister** is a lively refuge, with birds fluttering among the orange, magnolia, and palm trees and inhabited by 13 geese, symbolising the age of Eulàlia when she died. Watch where you walk, as the cloister is paved with tombstones, badly worn, but many still bearing the emblems of the bootmakers', tailors', and other craft guilds whose wealth helped pay for the cathedral. From the cloister, pass to the **Capella de Santa Llúcia,** a chapel with 13th- and 14th-century tombstones on the floor and a monument to a crusader knight in armour on one wall.

Leaving the chapel by its front entrance, turn left into Carrer del Bisbe. The corner house at No. 8 was until recently the official residence of the president of the Generalitat. Train your eyes upwards as you walk through the old town to take in the details – a curious hanging sign, a lantern, an unusual sculpture or an array of plants trailing from balconies. On the right is a row of gargoyles leaning from the roof of the **Palau de la Generalitat**, seat of the Autonomous Catalan government, where there is also a richly ornamented gateway. The lacy overhead bridge is Gothic in style but is actually a 1929 addition.

> Renditions of the *sardana*, the venerated Catalan folk dance, take place on Saturday evening and on Sunday at noon in front of the Cathedral. It is also performed in Plaça Sant Jaume on Sunday evening.

Just ahead is the spacious, serious **Plaça Sant Jaume,** the heart of the Barri Gòtic. A local joke says that the farthest distance in Barcelona is across this square, which separates the often antagonistic and conservative Generalitat from the more progressive municipal authorities in the Ajuntament (City Hall). Architecturally, though, the two buildings make a harmonious pair: both have classical façades that hide their Gothic origins. To visit either building, you'll need luck and planning; they can only be visited on public holidays such as 23 April (Sant Jordi), or at weekends by appointment *(see page 113)*.

The **Palau de la Generalitat,** on the north side of the square (closer to the Cathedral), is the more interesting of the two. This institution dates from 1359, when it was made the executive branch reporting to the parliament, the Corts Catalanes. The nucleus of the present building is the main patio – pure Catalan Gothic, with an open staircase leading to a gallery of arches on slender pillars. The building's star feature is the flamboyant Gothic façade of the **Capella de Sant Jordi.** The **Saló de Sant Jordi** (there's no escaping St George here), a large vaulted hall in the 17th-century front block of the building, is lined with modern murals of historical scenes.

The **Ajuntament,** or Casa de la Ciutat, across the plaza has held Barcelona's city hall since 1372. It was here that the Consell de Cent, a council of 100 notable citizens, met to deal with civic affairs under the watchful eyes of the king. The original entrance can be seen around the left corner of the building, on the Carrer de la Ciutat. Inside, the left staircase leads to the upper gallery of the old courtyard and to the **Saló de Cent** (Hall of the One Hundred). Its high ceiling resembles the barrel-vault of the Saló del Tinell *(see page 35)*, and was built at about the same time, in the 14th cen-

Gothic gargoyles look down on the activity below the Palau de la Generalitat.

tury. The red-and-yellow bars of Catalonia's flag decorate the walls. The hall where the city council now meets adjoins, and at the head of the black marble staircase is the **Saló de les Cròniques** (Hall of the Chronicles), noted for the modern murals in sepia tones by Josep Maria Sert.

From behind the Ajuntament, take the short Carrer d'Hèrcules to the **Plaça Sant Just** for a quick peek at the church of **Sants Just i Pastor** and the small, pretty square on which it sits, evocative of a bygone Barcelona. The church is one of the oldest in the city, though often remodelled. It is said that any will that has been sworn before its altar is recognised as valid by the courts of Barcelona, a practice dating from the 10th century.

Heading back to Plaça Sant Jaume, turn right on Carrer de la Llibreteria, a small street lined with pastry shops and one of Barcelona's oldest and tiniest coffee shops, El Mesón del Café. A couple of blocks down on the left, on Plaça del Rei is the **Museu d'Història de la Ciutat** (City History Museum). The building is a Gothic mansion that was moved stone by stone to this location. The chief attraction is in the basement, where excavations have uncovered the foundations, including sculptures, walls, a bathing pool, and cemeteries filled with remains of the Romans and Visigoths who once inhabited the city. On upper floors are maps of the Catalan empire, the original plans for the 19th-century expansion of the city that created the Eixample district, and other historical documents and artefacts. Visitors can also

Enjoying pastries from one of the many pastry shops on Carrer de la Llibreteria.

see a 28-minute "virtual history" multimedia film about Barcino-Barcelona.

From the museum it is only a step to the gorgeously austere **Plaça del Rei,** the courtyard of the **Palau Reial** (Royal Palace), which is dominated by the many-arched Renaissance tower of Rei Martí and the **Capella de Santa Àgata** (Chapel of St Agatha). Both can be visited on the same ticket as for the Museu d'Història.The chapel is notable for the 15th-century altarpiece of the *Adoration of the Magi* by one of Catalonia's finest artists, Jaume Huguet.

In the courtyard, the structure with the broad staircase is all that is left of the original Royal Palace of Catalonia, begun in the 10th century and added to over the years until it took up three sides of the square and extended to the rear. During the Inquisition, suspected heretics were burned at the stake in this enclosure, and here Ferdinand and Isabella received Columbus in 1493 on his return from his first voyage to the Americas. Columbus probably gave his report in the **Saló del Tinell.** This vast barrel-vaulted hall was built for royal audiences in 1359, and on occasion the Corts Catalanes (Parliament) met here. It was later used as a church. The palace's central section, chapel, and hall were recon-

Finding Your Way Around

Street addresses place the street number after the name, and the floor and apartment number after that. For example: Carrer Rosello, 28 3-4, means building number 28, third floor, apartment or office number 4. The abbreviation s/n stands for "*sin número*", or unnumbered.

Street, which is *Carrer* in Catalan, *Calle*, in Spanish is abbreviated "C/"; promenade or boulevard, *Passeig* (Pg.) or *Paseo* (Po); avenue, *Avinguda* (Avda.) or *Avenida* (Avda.).

structed between 1943 and 1952. Outdoor theatre and concert performances are held in the square in summer.

A former wing of the palace which encloses the Plaça del Rei was rebuilt in 1557 to become the **Palau del Lloctinent** (Palace of the Lieutenant), residence of the king's representative. Until recently it housed the Archives of Aragón. The entrance, reached by leaving the palace square and turning right on the Carrer dels Comtes, is an elegant patio with a noble staircase and remarkable carved wooden ceiling.

Just beyond, flanking the cathedral, is the **Museu Frederic Marès**, which has a beautiful courtyard. Marès, a 20th-century sculptor of civic statues, was a compulsive collector who bequeathed to Barcelona an unusually idiosyncratic collection of art and miscellany. The lower floors of the museum are stocked with Iberian votive figurines, Limoges enamel boxes, and religious sculptures from the 12th to the 19th centuries. You'll also find Portuguese carved ox yokes, a roomful of iron keys, old sewing machines, canes, wind-up toys – in short an endless catalogue of art and artefacts. There is even the suitcase, covered with travel stickers, which Marés used to cart home his loot.

Retracing your steps on the narrow street flanking the cathedral, circle around to the rear and duck into the narrow Carrer del Paradís. Here, just inside the doorway of the **Centre Excursionista de Catalunya,** four columns of the Roman Temple of Augustus are embedded in the wall.

Behind the Royal Palace, off Carrer Tapineria, is **Plaça de Berenguer el Gran,** which has a well-preserved section of the original Roman wall. The Roman defences were 9 metres (30 ft) high and 3.5 metres (12 ft) thick and marked at intervals by towers 18 metres (59 ft) tall. Until 1943, most of this section was covered by a clutter of old houses, which were dismantled and relocated to restore the walls to view.

The Plaça del Rei makes a good meeting place.

Since ancient times, when two main Roman thoroughfares intersected at the Plaça Sant Jaume, this has been the crossroads of Barcelona. Streets radiate in all directions, each an invitation to explore the Barri Gòtic. The Carrer del Call leads into the labyrinth of narrow streets that was the **Call,** or Jewish Quarter, until the Jews were killed, expelled or forcibly converted to Christianity late in the 14th century. Today the quarter is a bustling corner of antiques shops and dealers of rare books, plus bars and restaurants frequented by antiquarians and artists.

Although many of the streets retain the word Call in their names, there are few vestiges left of the ghetto, which once was surrounded by a wall. Barcelona's Jews, though noted as doctors, scholars, and jewellers, and despite their financing of the conquests of the crown, were confined to this district and forced to wear long, hooded cloaks with yellow headbands. Taxation of the community was a special source of royal income. This did not, however, save the Call from being burned and looted as persecution mounted in the 13th and 14th centuries. Just off Carrer del Call, at Carrer de Marlet 1, a medieval inscription in Hebrew marks the site of a hospital founded by one "Rabbi Samuel Hassareri, may his life never cease".

Nearby is the Baixada de Santa Eulàlia. Just off the street is **Plaça de Sant Felip Neri,** a tiny and silent square closed to traffic (silent except when children from the nearby school come out to play here). The saint's church was pockmarked by Italian bombs during the Civil War, though some maintain that firing squads performed executions here.

The Baixada de Santa Eulàlia descends to **Carrer dels Banys Nous,** named for the long-gone "new" baths of the ghetto erected in the 12th century. This winding street, which more or less follows the line of the old Roman wall, is the unofficial boundary of the Barri Gòtic. It is also known as the Carrer dels

Antiquaris – the street of antiques dealers. As you walk along, keep your eyes peeled for unusual hand-painted shop signs, the fretwork of Gothic windows, and dusty treasures in the antiques shop windows. You will see the old tile signs with a cart symbol high on the walls at some corners, the indication of one-way streets.

This moderniste bar on the pretty Plaça del Pi is a local landmark.

Around the corner is a trio of impossibly pretty plazas. **Plaça Sant Josep Oriol** adjoins **Plaça del Pi,** on which sits **Santa Maria del Pi,** a handsome church with a tall, octagonal bell tower and a harmonious façade pierced by a large 15th-century rose window. "Pi" means pine tree, and there is a small specimen here replacing one that was a landmark in past centuries.

Buildings in the Plaça del Pi show off the *sgrafitto* technique of scraping designs in coloured plaster, imported from Italy in the early 1700s. (Barcelona's emerging merchant class favoured such façades as an inexpensive substitute for the sculpture that was found in aristocratic palaces.)

> For three weeks in December, a market selling Nativity figurines occupies the *Plaça Nova* – a square that got its name, meaning "new," in 1356 and has held markets for nearly a thousand years. Look for the quintessential Catalan figure, *el caganer* – the red-capped peasant squatting and defecating beside the manger.

These adjoining squares, together with the smaller **Placeta del Pi** to the rear of the church, are the essence of old Barcelona and a great place to while away the hours. The bars with their tables spread out under leafy trees in each of the squares are magnets for young people and travellers, who are entertained by roving musicians. On Sunday, artists offer their canvases for sale in lively Plaça Sant Josep Oriol, where the Bar del Pi is a popular meeting place; and on Saturday and Sunday, dairy produce and honey are sold from stalls.

The street that leads north from Plaça del Pi, **Carrer Petritxol**, is one of the Barri Gòtic's most traditional. The narrow passageway is lined with art galleries, framing shops, and traditional *granjas* – good stops for pastries and hot chocolate. Barcelona's oldest, and most famous, art gallery is here: Sala Parés, at No. 5.

At Carrer Portaferrisa, a left turn will take you to La Rambla, while a right turn will take you back to the cathedral and a handful of additional sights on the perimeter of the Barri Gòtic. (You could also return to Plaça Sant Josep Oriol and take Carrer de la Palla). Back at Plaça Nova, in front of the cathedral is the modern **Col.legi d'Arquitectes** (College of Architects). Picasso designed the graffiti-like drawings of the Three Kings and the children bearing palm branches that are etched on the 1960s façade.

The busy pedestrian thoroughfare that leads north to Plaça de Catalunya is Avda Portal de l'Àngel, one of the city's main shopping streets. When there are *rebaixas*, or sales, happening, wading through the crowds here is no easy task. Look for the small Carrer Montsió, which leads to **Els Quatre Gats** (The Four Cats), a bar and restaurant that became famous when Picasso and a group of young bohemian intellectuals – the painters Ramón Casas and Santiago Rusiñol among them – began hanging out here. Picasso had his first public exhibition here in 1901, and the bar, one of the first commissions for the modernista architect Puig i Cadafalch, preserves its turn-of-the-century ambience.

LA RIBERA

Some of the most beautiful Gothic architecture and most fascinating medieval corners of Barcelona lie just outside the Barri Gòtic. To the east of the Via Laietana – a busy, traffic-filled avenue roughly parallel to the Ramblas, which was cut through the old city in 1859 to link the port with the modern centre – and below the Carrer de la Princesa, which intersects it at midpoint, is the atmospheric quarter called La Ribera. Here you'll find both the **Museu Picasso** and the majestic church of **Santa Maria del Mar**. Carrer Argenteria, once the avenue to the sea from the Royal Palace, cuts

*Santa María del Mar's impressive arches represent
the height of Catalan Gothic architecture.*

a diagonal swathe from Plaça del'Angel to the church. Begun in 1329 at the height of Catalonia's expansion as a Mediterranean power, Santa Maria del Mar is the greatest example of pure Catalan Gothic, with unadorned exterior walls, a sober façade flanked by three-tiered octagonal bell towers, and a large rose window over the portal.

The dimensions and extraordinary austerity of the interior are breathtaking. Fires set during the rioting of 1936 at the outbreak of the Civil War tragically consumed all the trappings of chapels, choir, and altar, leaving the interior stripped to its essence. The result is a capacious, lofty hall suffused with soft light from the stained-glass windows. Three tall naves are supported by slim, octagonal columns set 13 metres (43 ft) apart, and the dimensions of the interior are multiples of this distance, achieving a perfect symmetry. Behind the simple, modern altar, the columns branch high overhead into the arched vaulting of the apse. The acoustics

Open-air café tables in front of the old Mercat del Born, which is being converted into a huge library.

are excellent, best demonstrated by the frequent concerts held in the church and the voices of choirboys at mass.

The rear door of the church leads to the **Passeig del Born,** a plaza where jousts were held in the Middle Ages and which today is full of galleries, restaurants and clubs – very much the place to be. Many of the little streets surrounding the church are named for the craftsmen who once worked here: *Sombrerers* (hatmakers), *Mirallers* (mirror-makers), *Espartería* (makers of rope-soled shoes), and *Espasería* (sword-makers). Today the area is better known for the people who fill its bars late into the night and spill out onto the streets; disgruntled residents hang signs from their windows pleading with the municipal government to impose quiet hours.

One of Barcelona's grandest medieval streets, **Carrer Montcada,** populated by aristocrats from the 14th to the

16th centuries, is lined with Gothic palaces, each with an imposing door or arched gate to an inner courtyard from where an ornamental staircase usually led up to reception rooms. These mansions were gradually abandoned after the demolition of the adjoining district and construction of the Ciutadella fortress. The quarter around Santa Maria del Mar decayed gently without interference, leaving it the most authentically medieval part of the city.

The **Museu Picasso,** recently enlarged in grand fashion, now occupies five palaces (the latter two used for temporary exhibitions). The main entrance is through the 15th-century Palau Aguilar. the buildings were acquired by the city to house the collection of paintings, drawings, and ceramics donated by Picasso's lifelong friend and secretary, Jaume Sabartés. After the museum opened in 1963, Picasso added sketches and paintings from his childhood and youth. Barcelona's collection of Picasso's work is the largest outside Paris, where the artist lived and became internationally renowned after leaving Barcelona.

The earliest works date from Picasso's ninth year. As a teenager he produced large canvases in the moralising 19th-century realist manner, such as the *First Communion* and

---

Pablo Picasso

The world's most acclaimed 20th-century artist, Pablo (Pau) Ruiz y Picasso was born in 1881 in Málaga, the son of a drawing teacher whose work took the family to Barcelona. In 1900, Picasso visited Paris, and settled there four years later. Picasso never returned to Barcelona after 1934, and in any case his opposition to the Franco regime would have made it impossible. When Picasso died in 1973 the bulk of his own collection, now in the Musée Picasso in Paris, went to the French government in a deal to settle taxes.

No longer the ticket booth for the Palau de la Música Catalana, but still delightful.

Science and Charity. It appears that, as Picasso's talent developed, he digested the styles of the past and of his contemporaries, proved he could equal them, then forged ahead. The museum doesn't possess any of the master's finest works but it does have two good examples of his Blue Period (1901–4), as well as *The Harlequin* (1917), and the idiosyncratic *Las Meninas* series, the variations on the theme of the Velázquez masterpiece in Madrid's Prado Museum, which provides a fascinating view of Picasso's innovative and deconstructivist approach to his subject.

Across the street is the **Museu Tèxtil i de la Indumentària** (Textile and Costume Museum), in the former palace of the Marqueses de Llió. The collection brings to life the elegance enjoyed by the wealthy families who occupied the Montcada mansions. The costumes on display are of superb silks, satins, and furs, embroidered and stitched to perfection. Styles represented reach all the way to the flapper dresses of the 1920s.

The **Museu Barbier-Mueller,** in a 16th-century palace at Montcada 14, houses an interesting collection of pre-Colombian art. All of the mansions along this street merit a peek in at the courtyards, but one that's always open is the handsome, baroque **Palau Dalmases** at No. 20. On the ground floor is an over-the-top, rococo bar called Espai Barroc (meaning, appropriately, Baroque Space). At the end of the street is Plaçeta Montcada where the you can get wonderful Basque tapas in the Euskaletxea bar.

Between neighbourhoods, up via Laeitana several blocks from Carrer Princesa, is one of the city's greatest achievements of *modernista* architecture, the **Palau de la Música Catalana** (Sant Francesc de Paula 2). The Palace of Catalan Music, designed by Lluís Domènech i Montaner, may be the perfect (albeit chaotic) expression of *modernisme*, and has been designated a UNESCO World Heritage site. It is an explosion of mosaics, tiles, stained glass, enamel, sculpture, and carving – a wildly audacious outpouring of contours and colours. The brick exterior, with Moorish arches and columns inlaid with floral tile designs, is sober compared to what's inside.

Even though every square inch is embellished, right down to the tiles underfoot, the hall is not overpowering or claustrophobic. One of Domènech's main concerns was to let in as much natural light as possible, and the hall is indeed light and roomy. The structural skeleton is iron – an innovation in those days – which allows the walls to be made of glass. Sunlight streaming in during afternoon concerts sets the place on fire. On either side of the orchestra's stage the rich colours of the room are offset by two wildly sculpted groups of musical masters in white plaster. Between these fevered creations of the sculptor Pau Gargallo, Picasso's friend, the silvery pipes of a grand organ stand in orderly contrast.

Overhead is the Palau's crowning glory, a magical, stained-glass orb. Behind the musicians a curved wall is covered with mosaics of muses playing instruments, from bagpipes to castanets. Their upper bodies are made of porcelain and seem to emerge magically from the walls. This may all sound too much, but it has to be seen to be believed. The best way to experience the Palau is to attend a concert. The hall was built in 1908 for a musical society called the Orfeó Català, but today programmes range from top symphony orchestras and soloists to avant-garde pop-rock groups. Tickets may be purchased at the box office on Sant Pere Més Alt, near the top of Via Laietana. Guided tours, in English, Spanish, and Catalan are given daily from 10am to 3.30pm (Tel. 93/268 10 00). The recent demolition of the undistinguished church next the Palau is part of a long-awaited expansion plan and allows the exterior to be fully appreciated.

> The modern extension of Barcelona is almost always called the Eixample (eye-*shahm*-pluh), in Catalan, although some older citizens hold onto the Spanish name, El Ensanche (en-*sahn*-chay). It simply means enlargement and it is an innovative example of town planning, still admired by planners and architects today.

EL EIXAMPLE & MODERNISME

The Eixample, Barcelona's modern district north of Plaça de Catalunya, is the city's main shopping and banking area. It's where you'll want to spend a good portion of your time if you've been waiting for Gaudí. The neighbourhood is flush with spectacular apartment buildings, examples of the city's unique early 20th-century *modernista* architecture, and is called the **Quadrat d'Or** (Golden Square).

The principal shopping and strolling avenues are the elegant Passeig de Gràcia, Barcelona's version of the Champs d'Elysee, and the Rambla de Catalunya, an uptown segment of La Rambla. In a manageable area between the Gran Vía de les Corts Catalanes and Avinguda Diagonal, you'll find most of the *modernista* masterpieces. Two of Barcelona's signature sights, Gaudí's unfinished cathedral La Sagrada Família and his fantasy-land residential community, Parc Güell *(see pages 57–8)*, are on the northern outskirts of the Eixample (both easily accessible by taxi or metro, and the former is walkable).

Despite the exuberance of the architecture, the city's modern district is a model of rationalist urban planning, a rigid geometric grid simply called "the Extension". The outrageous and conservative coexist here without much fuss.

Barcelona's expansion came about in a remarkable burst of urban development. By the mid-1800s the city was bursting at the seams and suffocating inside its ring of medieval walls. A municipal competition was held in 1859 to select a plan for a new quarter between the old city and the Collserola hills. The job went to a road engineer named Ildefons Cerdà, whose plan quintupled the city's size in a matter of decades. The Eixample

"Cloud and Chair"– sculpture atop the Fundació Antoni Tàpies, the gallery dedicated to this artist's work.

The early 20th century saw an explosion of modernista architecture in Barcelona.

construction transformed the city into a showcase of extravagant *modernista* architecture, and the swanky Passeig de Gràcia became the place to be seen. Barcelona used the 1888 Universal Exposition as an open house to show the world its new face.

The place to begin a *modernista* tour is definitely on Passeig de Gràcia, with its single, hallucinatory block popularly known as the **Illa de la Discòrdia** (Block of Discord) between Consell de Cent and Aragó. It gained its name because of the three buildings in markedly different styles that stand almost next door to each other. Unfortunately, none of these three buildings is open to the public any more, but the exteriors are stunning and it is possible to see into the entrance halls. During 2002, International Gaudí Year, celebrating his 150th anniversary, it will be possible to visit some buildings not usually open to the public.

Domènech i Montaner's **Casa Lleó Morera** (1902–6), at No. 35, incorporates Moorish and Gothic elements. This grand corner apartment house has suffered the most disfigurement, especially on the ground floor, where the Spanish leather goods company Loewe installed picture windows and destroyed several original sculptures. The building now belongs to a publishing company.

Casa Amatller (1900), just up the block at No. 41, was built for a chocolate manufacturer. Puig i Cadafalch drew inspiration from Flanders for the stepped roof covered in glazed tiles. The Institut Amatller d'Art Hispànic on the top floor contains documents on Hispanic art and furniture by Puig i Cadafalch. The office that runs the Ruta del Modernisme *(see page 113)* is situated in this building, so you can get into the lobby to see the antique elevator and the wonderful staircase. The Ruta del Modernisme ticket allows

Modernisme

Modernisme, a movement related to the design styles in vogue in Europe in the late 19th century – French *Art Nouveau*, German and Austrian *Jugendstil* – was a rebellion against the rigid forms and colourless stone and plaster of classical architecture. In Barcelona the new style assumed nationalist motifs and significance. Its cultural importance may be the reason it has been so carefully preserved here.

Although there was an entire school of *modernista* architects working in Barcelona from the late 19th century until the movement's demise in the 1930s, it is customary to speak of the "Big Three". Antoni Gaudí, wildly creative, is the best-known, and he and Barcelona have become synonymous. The eccentric genius lived a long, productive life, and his work is found all over the city. Casa Milà, usually known as La Pedrera, is his finest work, closely followed by Casa Batlló, La Sagrada Família, and Parc Guëll. Lluís Domènech i Montaner (1850–1923), may have been the most accomplished of the group; he created the astonishing Palau de la Música Catalana *(see page 45)*, Hospital de Sant Pau, and Casa Lleó Morera. Josep Puig i Cadafalch (1867–1957) built Casa Amatller, turretted Casa de les Punxes (Casa Terrades) on Avda Diagonal and Els Quatre Gats *(see page 52)*.

reduced price entry to seven other buildings and shows you where to find *modernista* bars, shops and restaurants.

Gaudí's highly personal **Casa Batlló** (1904–6) is next door. The curvy contours, unexpected combinations of textures and materials, bright colours, and infinite detail are Gaudí hallmarks, as are his prevalent religious and nationalist symbolism. The Casa Batlló is said to pay tribute to the patron saint of Catalonia, Sant Jordi, and the dragon he

Gaudí

Perhaps no architect has left so personal a mark on a city as Antoni Gaudí did on Barcelona. His style is so much his own that he has not been the fount of a continuing school and now seems to have been the only one of his kind. A century later, one wonders how on earth he convinced conservative merchants and churchmen to accept his wildly imaginative ideas. Count Eusebi Güell, a textile manufacturer, was his patient and daring patron.

The Palau Güell, which Gaudí began in 1885, previews many aspects of Gaudí's work, in that it draws on styles of the past— Gothic and Moorish — and distorts them as a dream distorts reality. Gaudí was a talented designer of furniture and interior decorations, and he closely supervised every detail of the assignments he gave his artisans.

For all his innovations, Gaudí was a deeply pious and conservative man. He was also a defiant nationalist. He once insisted on speaking Catalan to the Spanish-speaking king, and when a client complained that there was no room for her piano in the music room he designed, Gaudí's response was "let her take up the violin". When passers-by discovered the architect run over by a tram in 1926 and took him to hospital the doctors, unable at first to identify him, thought he was a tramp. When they discovered who he was, the entire city turned out for his funeral.

valiantly slayed. Gaudí himself left no clues as to his intent. The undulating blue-tile roof indeed looks like a dragon's scaly hide, while the balconies could be the skulls and bones of its victims (others have suggested they are Venetian carnival masks). Sant Jordi's cross and a shaft suggest a spear being thrust into the dragon's back. Casa Batlló's façade is covered with scraps of broken plate and tile, a decorative technique called *trencadis* that Gaudí employed repeatedly. Gaudí did not build the entire house, but he was commissioned to remodel both the exterior and interior in 1906.

Farther up and across the street, at No. 92, is **Casa Milà** (1905–10), Gaudí's masterwork. Known as **La Pedrera** (Stone Quarry, an allusion to its rippling, limestone surface), this stunning apartment house is a UNESCO World Heritage Site. The sinuous façade with wonderfully twisted wrought-iron balconies bends around the corner of Carrer Provença. The building was

given a facelift in the mid-1990s, and it looks better than ever. The apartments inside had suffered unspeakable horrors, and Gaudí's beautiful arched attics had been sealed up, but today everything has been restored to its original state. The attic floor is now a handsomely re-alised, high-tech museum (called Espai Gaudí) with an interesting exhibition of his

The vibrant colours of Casa Batlló take on different tones at night.

Modernisme's Alternative Hits List

The major modernista sights near the Manzana de la Discòrdia on Passeig de Gràcia, in addition to the Sagrada Família and Parc Güell, are on everybody's list of essential sights. If you have time and interest for more, here's a second tier of *modernisme*'s greatest hits:

Antigua Casa Montaner i Simón (Fundació Antoni Tàpies) Domènech i Montaner, 1880-1885; *c/ Aragó, 255*

Casa Calvet Gaudí, 1898-1900; *c/ Casp, 48*

Casa Fuster Domènech i Montaner, 1908; *Passeig de Gràcia, 132*

Casa Planells Josep María Jujol, collaborator of Gaudí; *Avda. Diagonal, 332*

Casa Terrades (Casa de les Punxes) Puig i Cadafalch, 1903-1905; *Avda. Diagonal, 416*

Casa Thomas (B.D. Ediciones de Diseño) Domènech i Montaner, 1895-1898; *Mallorca, 291*

Casa Vicens Gaudí, 1883-1888; *c/ de les Carolines, 18-24*

Colònia Güell Gaudí; *outside Barcelona in Santa Coloma de Cervelló*

Hospital de la Santa Creu i Sant Pau Domènech i Montaner; *c/ Cartagena at Sant Antoni María Claret*

Hotel España Domènech i Montaner/Ramón Casas; *c/ Sant Pau, 9-11*

Palau Güell Gaudí, 1886–1890; *Nou de la Rambla 3-5*

Casa Quadras Puig i Cadafalch, 1904–1906; *Avda. Diagonal, 373*

Torre Bellesguard Gaudí, 1900-1904; *c/ Bellesguard, 16-20, in Sarrià*

work. First opened to the public in 1999 was one of the original apartments, all odd shapes, handcrafted doorknobs, and idiosyncratic details. It has been meticulously outfitted with period furniture, many of the pieces designed by Gaudí.

For many, though, the highlight is the wavy rooftop, with its cluster of swirling Darth Vader-like chimneys, known as "witch scarers", and spectacular views of Barcelona, all the way to the sea. La Pedrera had one of the world's first underground parking garages; today the space houses an ampitheatre where cultural conferences are held. The building's owner, the cultural foundation Fundació Caixa de Catalunya, has transformed the second floor into a sumptuous exhibition space for a variety of impressively curated shows (entrance is free). Tours of Casa Milà are given in English, Spanish, and Catalan, daily 10am–8pm, and they include access to the Espai Gaudí and rooftop (tel. 93-484 59 95). On summer weekend evenings between 8pm and midnight you can enjoy a variety of cocktails and jazz on the terrace.

You are likely to be busy looking up, or gazing in chic store windows, when you stroll along **Passeig de Gràcia,** but be sure to notice the ground as well: Gaudí himself designed the hexagonal pavement tiles with nature motifs. The mosaic benches and iron street lamps with little bats (1900) are by Pere Falqués.

Getting Around

Catalan	Spanish	English
Carrer	Calle	street
Avinguda (Avd.)	Avenida	avenue
Passeig (Pg)	Paseo (P)	boulevard
Plaça	Plaza	square
estació	estación	station
aeroport	aeropuerto	airport

Additional examples of *modernisme*, by these and other architects of the period, are littered throughout the Eixample and are too numerous to detail here (the list on page 52 highlights several of them). Have a look at Passeig de Gràcia to the east, especially the streets Diputació, Consell de Cent, Mallorca, and València as far as the Mercat de la Concepció market. In the old town you'll stumble across marvellous *modernista* store fronts, such as the Filatèlia Monge stamp shop at Carrer dels Boters 2, and the Antiga Casa Figueras bakery on the Ramblas; and there's the wonderful dining room of the Hotel España in Carrer Sant Pau – worth eating there for the decor alone.

If Barcelona's given you've the design bug, there are two excellent shops that specialise in design and are well worth a visit, as much for their contents as for the spectacular turn-of-the-century palaces that house them: **B.D. Ediciones de Diseño,** on Mallorca, 291; and **Vinçon,** housed in the mansion that once belonged to Picasso's contemporary, the painter Ramón Casas, at Passeig de Gràcia 96 *(see page 81)*.

In addition to the jewels of *modernista* architecture, **Passeig de Gràcia** *(Paseo de Gracia* in Spanish) is lined with outdoor cafés, cinemas, galleries, bookstores, and elegant fashion boutiques. This is definitely the place for designer shopping, as well as more down-to-earth fashion, such as that at Zara, the Spanish enterprise that has now become internationally known. A number of the top hotels are on or near this avenue.

The **Plaça de Catalunya,** where the boulevard begins, was designed to be the city's hub, and it certainly is lively, if not the most attractive space in Barcelona. The bus, metro, and the regional and national rail systems radiate from this square and El Corte Inglés department store occupies the whole of the northern side.

Ornate wrought-iron street lamps, dating from the early 1900s, are a feature of Passeig de Gràcia.

Parallel to **Passeig de Gràcia** is an extension of the Old Town Ramblas, the **Rambla de Catalunya**. It is lined with smart shops, tapas bars, restaurants and galleries. Traffic moves down either side, but the centre is pedestrian-only and is considerably more sedate than the lower Ramblas.

On Carrer d'Aragó between Passeig de Gràcia and Rambla de Catalunya is the **Fundació Antoni Tàpies,** a gallery dedicated to the work of Spain's foremost living artist, the abstract materialist from Catalonia. In addition to Tàpies's work, the Fundació has interesting changing international exhibitions, but at least half the reason to visit is to see the gorgeous 1880 Domènech i Montaner building in which it is all housed. Built for the publishers Montaner i Simón, this is one of the first examples of modernisme. From outside you can appreciate Tàpies' whimsical, tangled wire sculpture *Núvol i Cadira* ("Cloud and Chair") on the roof.

☞ La Sagrada Família

What the Eiffel Tower is to Paris or the Statue of Liberty is to New York, the soaring spires of the Sagrada Família church are to Barcelona. Its unmistakable profile, protruding from the city's skyline, is visible from afar. Yet the eight peculiar, cigar-shaped towers are merely the shell of a church that was begun in 1882 and is still many years from completion. This was Antoni Gaudí's life work, though he didn't really expect to finish it in his lifetime.

For many years, the church remained much as it was when Gaudí died, but a foundation is now trying to complete the building—not an easy task, since Gaudí left few detailed plans behind. You can ascend one of the towers (by lift or narrow spiral staircase) for an overview.

Gaudí, who died in 1926 at the age of 74, is buried in the crypt. During his last years he lived in a room on the site, obsessed with the project. As indisputably original as church is, it was not Gaudí's work from the very start. He took over the more traditional, neo-Gothic plans of an earlier architect and supervised work on the eastern Nativity (Nacimiento) façade, one tower, and part of the apse and nave.

The western Passion (Pasión) façade and its towers have been under construction since 1952, with builders using plans by other architects emulating his style. The east façade shows best what Gaudí intended. Everything has significance and a name, and no space is left unfilled. The three doorways, with stonework dripping like stalactites, represent Faith, Hope, and Charity, and are loaded with sculptures depicting angel choirs and musicians, and Biblical episodes such as the birth and youth of Jesus, the Flight into Egypt, the Slaughter of the Innocents, the Tree of Calvary, and much more. The cathedral is intended to incorporate every aspect of creation and faith.

Twelve towers, four at each portal, represent the Apostles; four higher ones, the Evangelists; a dome over the apse, the Virgin; and the central spire, the Saviour.

Many people believe the temple should have been left as it was, unfinished, as a tribute to the great Gaudí, but onward it goes, the work supervised by Jordi Bonet Armengol, son of one of Gaudí's aides. Work on the Nacimiento façade is by Japanese sculptor, Etsuro Sotoo, and even those who opposed it agree that it is remarkably in keeping with Gaudí's ideas. When it will all be finished, nobody knows. For now, the great spires are marred by ever-present scaffolding and cranes.

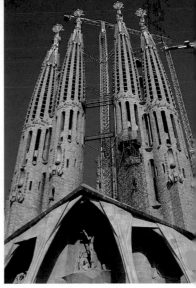

La Sagrada Família's soaring spires and cranes.

A short walk diagonally from La Sagrada Família, along Avinguda de Gaudí, is the astonishing **Hospital de la Santa Creu i Sant Pau**, designed by Domènech i Montaner and completed by his son. The complex of buildings–still a working hospital–is one of *modernisme*'s most underrated (and least known) achievements. Visitors can wander through the grounds and admire the structures from outside.

Farther north, in a working class neighbourhood on the rising slope of the hills behind Gràcia, **Parc Güell,** another wildly ambitious Gaudí project, was planned as a residential community, to be completely intertwined with nature. Although it was never completed, it is a marvellous place to visit, part park, part fantasy land. Gaudí's patron Eusebi Güell bought 6 ha (15 acres) here, overlooking the city and the sea, intending to create a community of villas. He gave Gaudí carte blanche to produce something original, and for the next 14 years, on and off, the architect delighted in letting his imagination run wild. A gingerbread gatehouse guards the entrance on the Carrer d'Olot; a tiled lizard fountain gurgles water from its jaws; supporting columns mimic tree trunks. Ceilings are decorated with broken fragments of plates, and wildly undulating benches are splashed with dizzying colourful ceramic pieces, Gaudí's beloved *trencadís*, although much of the work was done by Josep Maria Jujol.

Beneath the plaza with the benches is the **Saló de les Cent Columnes** (Hall of the One Hundred Columns). There actu-

The rainbow hues of a mosaic bench at the Parc Güell, one of the most-visited sights in Barcelona.

ally are 86, Doric in style, in what was to be the colony's covered market. Look closely at the ceiling and you'll see dolls' heads, bottles, glasses, and plates stuck in the mosaics.

Only five buildings were completed. Gaudí lived for many years in one, which is now the Casa-Museu Gaudí, a museum of his furniture and other memorabilia.

WATERFRONT & BARCELONETA

Barcelona turned its back on the sea in the 19th century and focused on developing industry. The sea wall where families loved to walk and catch the breeze on stifling summer nights was dismantled. Access to the sea was obstructed by warehouses and railway tracks and expansion proceeded towards the hills. Barceloneta, a neighbourhood created in the early 18th century between the port and the beach as part of a military initiative, remained a close-knit working-class community. But things have changed with the creation of an ambitious recreational and commercial area along the waterfront.

Begin a tour of the waterfront at the Columbus Monument, at the foot of the Ramblas. To the right is Les Reials Drassanes, begun in 1255, the only medieval shipyard still in existence and now housing the **Museu Marítim** (Maritime Museum). The 16 bays of these yards, which could once handle more than 30 galleys at a time, launched ships that extended Catalonia's dominion over the Mediterranean from Tunis to Greece, Sicily, Sardinia, and much of the French coast. The museum contains models of ships, from the earliest galleys to the cargo and passenger ves-

Golondrinas

A perennial waterfront attraction are the ferries called *Golondrinas* (Swallows), moored opposite the Columbus Monument, which have been taking passengers round the harbour ever since the 1888 World Exposition.

Luxury yachts line the quays of the Port Vell.

sels, that have made Barcelona their home port up to the present day. The prize exhibit is the full-size copy of the Royal Galley, *La Reial*, aboard which Don Juan of Austria commanded the fleet that defeated the Turks at the Battle of Lepanto in 1571. The museum has restored an early 20th-century cargo vessel, the *Santa Eulàlia*, which sits in the harbour and can be visited.

At the other side of the busy Passeig de Colom is an undulating wooden walkway and footbridge (mind your step, it's easy to trip) called the Rambla del Mar. Designed as an extension of the Ramblas and popular with Sunday strollers, it crosses over to the **Moll d'Espanya** and leads to **Maremàgnum,** a commercial centre with an Imax cinema, lots of shops (open late), bars, discos and restaurants. It's mostly of fast food in the latter, but it's a great place to sit and watch the activity in the harbour. Families often head for **L'Aquárium de Barcelona**; one of Europe's largest aquariums, its main attraction is a spectacular glass tunnel on the sea bed.

The port is busy with boats from the Royal Yacht Club, cruise ships, and ferries to Mallorca. Overhead, **cable cars** link Montjuïc with the Torre de Jaume I and the Torre de Sant Sebastià in Barceloneta. The World Trade Center, a complex of offices designed by I. M. Pei on the end of the Moll de Barcelona, appears to be floating in the harbour.

On the mainland, the **Moll de la Fusta,** the old wood-loading quay, was transformed into a broad promenade in the 1980s, planted with palms and lined with restaurants and clubs. The project proved unsuccessful, however, probably due to the noise and fumes from the traffic-filled waterfront highway, and it is now being redesigned. There is a large underground car park beneath it.

Heading towards Barceloneta, you reach the **Marina Port Vell** (Old Port) now transformed into a harbour for luxury yachts and motor cruisers. On the **Moll de Barceloneta**, in a renovated warehouse complex, is the **Museu d'Història de Catalunya**, which is fun as well as informative. Beneath it, and all along the Passeig Joan de Borbó that parallels the quay, are numerous popular restaurants, with outside tables.

Barceloneta

Those who want to eat really good fish head into **Barceloneta**, "Little Barcelona", an area or many years separated from the city as much in spirit as by the physical barriers of water and rail yards. It was built in the early 18th century to house dispossessed families when La Ribera district was demolished to make way for the Ciutadella fortress. A robust *barrio* inhabited by fishermen's families, its beaches were scruffy and dominated by flimsy wooden restaurants, *chiringuitos* (shacks).

When the area was virtually rebuilt in preparation for the 1992 Olympics, they were wiped out, and many Barceloneses nostalgically mourn their loss. You can cut through the grid of narrow streets or walk along the beach to the landscaped Passeig Marítim and the Platja Barceloneta, where wooden walkways and scrupulously clean sandy beaches attract local residents and visitors. The promenade was ravaged by storms in 2001 but are being extensively renovated.

Frank Gehry's giant copper fish has become one of the symbols of the new Barcelona.

Keep walking and you will come to the 1992 athletes' Olympic Village, the **Vila Olímpica**, an award-winning development that has blossomed into a smart and vibrant neighbourhood for young families and professionals. It is recognisable from afar by two high-rise buildings – one the prestigious **Hotel Arts** – and Frank Gehry's enormous, shimmering copper fish. As you approach, passing a small park, the gleaming Hospital de Mar, and a *modernista* water tower, the promenade becomes increasingly lined with bars and restaurants. Here and in the **Port Olímpic**, just beyond, there are a few good places to eat, and the proximity to beaches and boats is undeniably attractive, but the area has become over-commercialised and a bit tacky.

Beyond the Olympic Port, development continues. There are more clean, sandy beaches, and the old factories of **Poble Nou** district have been transformed into studios and apartments. Further still, **Diagonal Mar**, a project to bring the

Avinguda Diagonal down to the sea, has created a new district, demolishing old buildings and transforming wasteland. It's unfinished, but growing fast. A zoological park, exhibition areas and a port are underway as part of the Universal Forum of Cultures to be held here in 2004.

Lodged between Port Olímpic and La Ribera district is **Parc de la Ciutadella**, the city's largest park, which incorporates the city zoo, the **Parc Zoológic**. This was the site, first, of the fortress built after the fall of Barcelona in 1714, and then of the 1888 World Exposition. Housed in splendid *modernista* buildings designed for this event are the Zoological and Geological Museums, the Modern Art Museum, the seat of the Catalan Parliament. It's a lovely park, with an artificial lake, and towering trees. The large baroque fountain, La Cascada, was designed by Josep Fontseré, whose assistant was a young architecture student named Antoni Gaudí.

The main attraction of the **Museu d'Art Modern** is its collection of 19th- and early 20th-century Catalan works, particularly those of the Modernist school. There are some notable canvases by Santiago Rusiñol and Ramón Casas and an interesting collection of furniture and decorative arts.

From the park's northwest (inland) exit a broad promenade passes the old

The ornate fountain on which Gaudí worked when he was a student.

Santa Catalina market place and leads to the imposing **Arc de Triomf**, built as the entrance to the World Exposition. On the sea side of the park, in the area between La Ribera and the harbour, lie the grand and newly renovated Estació de França; the emblematic "Barcelona Head" sculpture by Roy Lichtenstein; the huge and ornate Correus (Post Office); and **La Llotja,** a centre of Barcelona's trading activities for more than 600 years. The building served variously as a Chamber of Commerce, a School of Fine Arts (where Picasso and Miró studied) and the Barcelona Stock Exchange (which is now in Passeig de Gràcia). You can sometimes visit the building (tel: 93 319 2412).

EL RAVAL

The district between La Rambla and the Ronda de Sant Antoni, once the line of the city wall, is **El Raval**, a neighbourhood being rapidly renovated, with numerous old buildings demolished to create open spaces. Start on the Ramblas, taking Carrer del Carme, then turn right up Carrer del Àngels to reach the most conspicuous symbol of the transformation of this neighbourhood: Richard Meier's shockingly modern, and blindingly white **Museu d'Art Contemporani de Barcelona** (MACBA). Erected as a controversial counterpoint to the rest of the delapidated *barrio*, the museum is worth visiting for its architecture alone. It is still working on putting together a serious contemporary collection but has some fine works and temporary exhibitions.

Next door, on Carrer Montalegre, is the **Centre de Cultura Contemporània de Barcelona** CCCB, a striking modern makeover of an old poor house, the Casa de Caritat. Dance, music, film and video presentations posit Barcelona, or the urban experience, as their theme. Retrace your steps now to Carrer del Carme and the Gothic complex of the

The streamlined MACBA building is evidence
of Barcelona's continual evolution.

Hospital de la Santa Creu (Hospital of the Holy Cross), a hospital and refuge for pilgrims for a thousand years. Gaudí died here in 1926. The present structures were begun in 1401. Look for the frieze of 16th-century tiles on the life of St Paul in the entryway of the **Institut d'Estudis Catalans.** The courtyard is restful, with benches under orange trees ripe with fruit in summer. Exhibitions of art and books are held in halls off the cloister.

Carrer Hospital is a busy commercial street catering to the Pakistani families in the area. On and around it are some trendy little shops and restaurants, although the alleys are not very inviting. On the far side of Hospital, the brand new Rambla del Raval leads down to Carrer Sant Pau. Old housing was demolished to make way for it, and new blocks are being built as part of the urban regeneration process.

Off in a corner at the end of Carrer Sant Pau is the little church of **Sant Pau del Camp**. The simplicity of its 12th-century Romanesque lines is an agreeable change from the extravagance of Barcelona's modernisme and the intricacies of Gothic architecture. It is believed to be the oldest church in the city and incorporates parts of a church begun in 912. The lovely little cloister has curious, Arab-style arches. The church is often locked. To see the interior, try late weekday afternoons (5–7.30pm), or Sunday morning.

MONTJUÏC

Montjuïc was the natural site for the core events of the 1992 Olympic Games. For many years its 210-metre (689-ft) summit, panoramic view of the city and harbour, and outstanding complex of museums and sports facilities have made the hill a favourite place to spend an afternoon.

Fountains play outside the Palau Nacional which houses the splendid Museu Nacional d'Art de Catalunya.

Montjuïc came into its own as the site of Barcelona's 1929 International Exhibition. The **Plaça d'Espanya's** ornate fountain was created to grace the entrance to the fairground and is still a good point to begin a visit to Montjuïc, as it has a metro and bus stop. A number of hangar-type halls, the premises of the Barcelona Trade Fairs organisation, line a

> In Roman times a road ran from the Mont Tàber citadel to Mons Jovis, which some believe was named for the god Jupiter. Others claim the origin is Mons Judaicus, "Hill of the Jews," named for a Jewish cemetery found on its slopes.

central pedestrian avenue leading upwards to the vast **Palau Nacional,** the fair's Spanish pavilion.

There are external elevators making the ascent easier to this domed palace, which holds one of the world's finest collections of medieval art, the **Museu Nacional d'Art de Catalunya.** Unmatched for Romanesque art and Gothic painting of the Catalan school, it has undergone extensive refurbishment; there are plans to house the Museum of Modern Art here eventually. Between the 9th and 13th centuries, more than 2,000 Romanesque churches were built in Catalonia, with thick, bare walls and rounded arches. Interiors were decorated with frescoes in the Byzantine tradition: primitive sculptures of biblical episodes or rural life on the capitals of columns; painted altar panels; carved wooden crosses, and Madonnas of great purity. Around the start of the 20th century many of these works were removed from churches that were deteriorating or abandoned, thus saving them from further damage or being sold out of the country.

Some of Spain's very best works of art are in this museum, such as the great 12th-century *Cristo Pantocrator* from the apse of the church of Sant Climent de Taüll in the Pyrenees. A superb group of unpainted, elongated wooden figures representing the descent from the cross is from the church of Santa Maria de Taüll. There are masterpieces in every room. The Gothic wing is excellent, too. Many of the paintings are *retablos*, screens with Gothic-arched frames that stood behind chapel altars. Among the treasures are Lluís Dalmau's *Virgin of the Councillors* (1445); Jaume Ferrer II's stylishly hatted *St. Jerome*; and a fine retable of St John the Baptist with saints Sebastian and Nicholas.

Up the hill and across the street is the **Museu Arqueològic** (Archaeological Museum). Among the exhibits, drawn mainly from prehistoric, Iberian, Greek, and Roman sites in Catalonia, are reconstructions of tombs and life-like dioramas. Around another curve, within walking distance up the hill, is the **Museu Etnològic** (Ethnological Museum). This well-presented collection usually has a special rotating programme highlighting the native arts of Latin America.

Farther up Montjuïc, turn left where the Avinguda de l'Estadi (the Olympic Ring boulevard) becomes the Avinguda de Miramar, to see the simple and elegant **Fundació Joan Miró.** The museum was designed in 1975 by the architect Josep Lluís Sert to house a large collection of paintings, drawings, tapestries and sculpture by the Catalan surrealist, who died in 1983 at the age of 90. The exhibits follow Miró's artistic

---

Leading to the Palau Nacional is the terrace of the *Font Màgica*, "Magic Fountain". On summer weekend evenings, from 8pm to midnight, the fountains perform a ballet of rising and falling jets bathed in a mist of changing colours programmed to music. People relax under the trees to listen or wander about with ice-cream cones while the flash bulbs of cameras wink like fireflies. Illuminated fountains rise on both sides of the central avenue down to the Plaça d'Espanya, and above the city the lights of Tibidabo shine like a beacon.

development from 1914 onwards. Flooded with natural light, they are seen at their best. In the grounds outside are a number of his sculptures. The collection is witty and bright with the unique language symbols associated with the artist.

Avinguda de Miramar continues past the station of the funicular that climbs the hill from Avinguda del Paral.lel (near the metro stop). The funicular links up with a cable car that goes to the **Castell de Montjuïc** and the Plaça de la Mirador on the summit. Cable cars run daily in summer, weekends only in winter.

There are sculptures on the terrace outside the Miró Foundation.

The fortress atop Montjuïc, built in 1640, remained in use by the army and then as a prison until shortly before it was turned over to the cityand converted into a museum in 1960. The **Museu Militar** (Military Museum) has an extensive collection of antique weaponry and armour, lead soldiers of different epochs, and models of Catalan castles. The fort has sombre associations for the city: its cannons bombarded the population to put down rebellions in the 18th and 19th centuries, and it was the site of political executions, including that of Lluís Companys, president of the Generalitat of Catalonia during the Civil War, who was shot by a firing squad in 1940.

The **Anella Olímpica** (Olympic Ring) spreads across the hillside on the northern side of Montjuïc and can be reached by escalator from the Palau Nacional. The 1929 stadium, now called **Estadi Olímpic,** was enlarged for the 1992 Games. Most of the track events and the opening and closing ceremonies were held here, and there's a Galeria Olímpica at the rear. Below the stadium is the Olympic Terrace; below that is the colonnaded Plaça d'Europa.

Off to the left is the handsome, high-tech **Palau d'Esports Sant Jordi**, designed by Japanese architect Arata Izozaki. It can seat 17,000 under a roof 45 metres (148 ft) high. Towering over it all is the 188-metre (616-ft) tall Torre de Calatrava communications tower. It caused great controversy when it was built but is now part of the landscape.

The **Poble Espanyol** (Spanish Village), on Montjuïc's northeastern flank, is a "fun for the whole family" attraction. Built for the Universal Exposition, it's a composite of architecture representing Spain's varied regions, including replicas of houses, church towers, fountains, plazas, and palaces arranged along a network of streets, alleys and village squares. The entrance is through one of the gates of the walled city of Ávila. There is a flamenco show and demonstrations of regional crafts. It's a bit cheesy and full of tourbus crowds, but it gives you a notion of the different regions of Spain, and there's plenty to entertain children.

Before you leave Montjuïc, visit the **Pabelló Mies van der Rohe,** a pavilion built for the 1929 Expo by the German minimalist, dismantled, then rebuilt again in 1986. The glass, stone, and steel cube house is a wonder of cool Bauhaus forms, tucked in the trees just off Avinguda Marqués de Comillas. Opposite is **Casaramona**, a former textile factory that has become the Caixa Forum, a cultural centre designed by Isozaki for the Fundació la Caixa.

THE DIAGONAL

The broad, tree-lined Avinguda Diagonal slices across Cerdà's grid from the coast to the hills. Designed for through traffic, it links up with the ring roads around the city and the toll highways beyond. The area around the **Plaça de les Glòries Catalanes,** a busy roundabout linking main roads into the city, was largely industrial, but is now the site of Ricardo Bofill's neoclassical Teatre Nacional de Catalunya and L'Auditori, designed by Rafael Moneo as the new home of the Barcelona Orchestra. Heading west, between the Passeig de Gràcia and the Plaça de Francesc Macià, is one of Barcelona's most elegant districts, with four-star hotels and luxury shops. Pricy restaurants and chic discos and clubs abound in adjoining streets.

A couple of miles further west along the Diagonal (there are frequent buses), is the **Palau Reial de Pedralbes,** an estate of the Güell family converted into a royal residence in 1919 in case King Alfonso XIII should drop by. It stands in a peaceful garden and houses two museums, the **Museu de les Artes Decoratives** (Museum of Decorative Arts) and the **Museu de Ceràmica** (Ceramics Museum).

Signs

Catalan	Spanish	English
entrada	entrada	entrance
sortida	salida	exit
lavabos/serveis	lavabos/servicios	toilet
arribada	llegada	arrival
sortida	salida	departure
rebaixes	rebajas	sale
fumadors	fumadores	smoker
no fumadors	no fumadores	non-smoker
tancat	cerrado(a)	closed
obert	abierto(a)	open

The districts on the hillside beyond were once separate villages where residents of Barcelona town often spent summers and weekends. They've been gradually absorbed over the years by Barcelona's expansion, but each preserves its own character. **Gràcia,** for example, has its own town square, the Plaça Rius i Taulet, and streets named Llibertat and Fraternitat and a Plaça Revolució, reflecting a political past. There's a great fiesta held here for a week around 15 August. **Sarrià** retains the feel of a small Catalan town, while the atmosphere of **Pedralbes** is patrician–residential villas with gardens and the city's most expensive real estate. The peaceful **Monestir de Pedralbes**, founded in 1326 has a superb Gothic church and a beautiful three-storey cloister. Part of the excellent **Thyssen-Bornemisza Collection**, including important medieval, Renaissance and baroque works is housed here (the major part of the collection is in the Thyssen museum in Madrid).

☞ TIBIDABO

The first bright, clear morning or late afternoon of your visit, head for **Tibidabo**, the 542-metre (1,778-ft) peak of the Collserola range, overlooking the city. The views are breathtaking. You can clearly make out the Sagrada Família and the grid plan of the Eixample. The church of the **Sagrat Cor**, floodlit at night, surmounted by a monumental figure of Christ, is one of the city's landmarks.

To reach the summit take the FGC train to Avda Tibidabo from the Plaça de Catalunya. From here a Tramvia Blau, an old-fashioned blue wooden tram, runs every day in summer, weekends in winter, taking you up to the funicular station, past stately mansions. En route, you could stop at the **Museu de la Ciència**, a splendid science museum that is being renovated at present (ask at a local tourist office if it has re-opened when you visit). In five

Palau Reial de Pedralbes in one of Barcelona's most exclusive neighbourhoods.

minutes the funicular (closed mid-October to February) lifts you through pine woods to the top, where you have a spectacular panorama of the city, the coast and, on very clear days, both Mallorca and the Pyrenees.

Tibidabo, and the famous, 1950s-style **Parc d'Atraccions** funfair, are just the best-known features of the **Parc de Collserola**, a huge, green swathe that makes a great escape from the city. Families come here at weekends and on summer evenings to enjoy the fresh air. There are jogging and cycling tracks, nature trails, picnic spots and *merenderos*, open-air restaurants where you barbecue your own food – hugely popular on summer Sundays. Another high spot is the **Torre de Collserola**, communications tower, also know as the Torre Foster, after the English architect Sir Norman Foster who designed it for the 1992 Olympics. It is open till 8pm, and a transparent lift will whisk you to the top for for panoramic views.

EXCURSIONS

There's an awful lot to detain you in Barcelona, but just beyond the city are several sites eminently worthy of day trips, including the holy Catalan shrine of Montserrat, the relaxed town of Sitges, for beaches and museums, and the *cava* wine country in the region of Penedès.

 ## Montserrat

Montserrat, Catalonia's most important religious retreat and the shrine of Catalan nationhood rises out of the rather featureless Llobregat plain 48 km (30 miles) northwest of Barcelona. The view from its 1,235-metre (4,050-ft) summit can encompass both the Pyrenees and Mallorca, and the monastery itself can be seen from afar, surrounded by jagged ridges which give it its name – "Serrated Mountain".

The first hermitages on the mountain may have been established by those trying to escape the Moorish invasion. One was enlarged as a Benedictine monastery in the 11th century and a century later it became the repository for **La Moreneta,** the Black Madonna, a small, wooden image of a brown-faced Virgin holding the infant Jesus on her lap and a globe in her right hand. The figure is said to be a carving by St Luke, later hidden by St Peter. Ever since, pilgrims—from commoners to kings – have climbed the mountain to worship the Catalan patron saint. More than a million pilgrims and tourists visit the shrine each year.

Like Catalan nationalism, the monastery has been destroyed only to rise again. It was burned to the ground by Napoleon's soldiers in 1808, abandoned in 1835 when all convents were sequestered by the state, and rebuilt in 1874. During the Spanish Civil War, when violent anti-clerical feelings were high among the Republicans in Barcelona, La Moreneta was secretly replaced by a copy; the original remained hidden during the dictatorship. Although Catalan culture was suppressed, monks here continued to say masses in Catalan.

The site of the monastery is spectacular, tucked into folds of rock high above the plain. On the eve of the saint's day, 27 April, the monks hold an all-night vigil attended by huge crowds. La Moreneta looks down from a gold-and-glass case, above and to the right of the altar in the basilica, but the faithful can touch or kiss her right hand through an opening. At 1pm and 7pm (except in July), the *Escolans*, the oldest boys' choir in Europe, founded in the 13th century, fill the basilica with their pure voices. The monastery and its museum contain many valuable works of art, include paintings by El Greco.

The monastery at Montserrat has great cultural significance for Catalans.

Montserrat is also the goal of outdoor sports pilgrims, like the cyclists (who make the trip from Barcelona) and mountain climbers who ascend the spires of rock above the building. From the monastery there are walks to other hermitages and a funicular to the cave sacred to the legend of the Madonna. Statues and plaques line the paths. Montserrat is an extremely popular place, so there are several bars and restaurants set up to feed the hordes.

Montserrat can be reached in spectacular fashion by FGC train from Barcelona's Plaça d'Espanya. On arrival at the Montserrat station (the journey takes about an hour), a cable car continues right up the side of the mountain to the monastery. There is also a bus service from Barcelona by Transportes Julià (tel: 93-490 40 00). If you are driving, leave Barcelona via the Diagonal and take the highway, direction Tarragona, exiting at Sortida 25.

Sitges

It's easy to get to the Costa Daurada beaches from Barcelona. The coast south of the city earned its name from its broad, golden sands, in contrast to the rocky coves of the Costa Brava to the north. Sitges, a favourite resort of Barceloneses, is the best place for a day trip. It's a short drive on the C-32 motorway, or a 40-minute train ride from the city's Estació Sants, if you get a fast train – some of them stop frequently en route. There is also scenic coastal drive that is narrow and curvy and obviously takes longer. Happily, the pretty little town has escaped the high-rises and tawdry atmosphere of many coastal resorts, although it does get somewhat overwhelmed by crowds in summer. There are two beaches, separated by a

Sunbathers flock to Sitges' beaches in high summer.

promontory where gleaming, whitewashed houses cluster around the church of Sant Bartomeu i Santa Tecla. The biggest and best is **Platja d'Or**, backed by a palm-lined promenade and dozens of cafés and restaurants – some of them very good.

> **At Corpus Christi in mid-June the streets of Sitges are carpeted with flowers. A solemn procession over them crushes the blooms and releases their scents.**

Besides the beaches, Sitges is known for its appealing museums. The **Museu Cau Ferrat** is in the house of the painter Santiago Rusiñol (1861–1931), whose collection of works by El Greco, Casas, Picasso, and others is on display, along with many of his own works. Across the street is the **Museu Maricel**, a splendid house overlooking the sea. In rooms decorated with painted tiles it displays a small collection of medieval sculpture and paintings, and some notable murals by Josep Maria Sert (1876–1945).

The nearby **Museu Romàntic** (on Sant Gaudenci) displays the furniture and accoutrements of a wealthy 19th-century family, as well as a large collection of antique dolls.

On the outskirts of Sitges are the villas of wealthy Barcelona families, while the narrow, pretty streets between the beach and station are geared for food and fun. Sitges has one of Spain's largest gay communities, and is a magnet for gay travellers year-round, but particularly during February *carnaval*. Gay and nudist beaches lie just beyond the town beaches.

Sant Sadurní d'Anoia (Penedès)

Cava, Catalonia's sparkling wine, comes from Penedès, a pretty spot south of Barcelona (about 45 minutes on the train from Sants or Plaça de Catalunya stations; by road, take the A7/E15 in the direction of Tarragona). These days the top-selling sparkling wine (which cannot be called champagne outside that region) is Catalan *cava* – Cordoníu and Freixenet. The main town in the grape-growing region is Sant Sadurní d'Anoia, where several top wineries offer guided tours and tastings.

The most interesting is **Codorníu,** Spain's largest producer of *cava*, who have been in the business since 1872. The family-owned winery is located on a spectacular campus, with buildings by Gaudí's contemporary, Puig i Cadafalch. Completed in 1898, it has been declared a National Artistic and Historic Monument. Visitors are taken on a theme-park-like ride through 26 km (16 miles) of atmospheric underground cellars. The winery is open year-round (except Christmas and New Year's Day), and guided visits in English are free during the week.

There are several good restaurants in and near town, which the staff at Codorniu will be happy to tell you about. Most specialise in seafood accompanied, of course, by *cava*. If you visit between January and March you must try another re-

gional dish, *calçots* – baby leeks grilled and dipped in a peppery, garlicky sauce.

Some 15 km (8 miles) south of Sant Sadurní, surrounded by extensive vineyards, is **Vilafranca del Penedès**, where the renowned Torres red wine is made. The excellent Museu del Vi can be visited.

Sant Sadurní d'Anoia is the place to sample cava.

Museums and Attractions

Casa Milà (La Pedrera), Passeig de Gràcia 92/Provença 261, tel: 93-484 59 95. Daily 10am–8pm. Guided tours available but not obligatory.

Catedral de Barcelona, Plaça de la Seu, s/n; tel: 93-315 15 54. Daily 8am–1.30pm and 4–7.30pm.

Fundació Joan Miró, Parc de Montjuïc, tel: 93-329 19 08. Tues, Wed, Fri & Sat 10am–7pm, Thurs 10am–9.30pm, Sun 10am–2.30pm.

Fundació Tàpies, Carrer de Aragó, tel: 93-488 01 39. Tues–Sun 11am–8pm.

L'aquàrium (Barcelona Aquarium), Moll d'Espanya del Port Vell, tel: 93-221 74 74. Summer daily 9.30am–11pm; winter 9.30am–9pm.

Museu d'Art Contemporani de Barcelona (MACBA), Plaça del Àngels, tel: 93-412 08 10. Mon, Wed–Fri, 11am–7.30pm; Sat 10am–8pm; Sun and holidays 10am–3pm.

Museu d'Art Modern, Parc de la Ciutadella, tel: 93-423 71 99 (as for MNAC). Tues–Sat 10am–7pm, Sun 10am–2.30pm.

Museu d'Història de la Ciutat (City History Museum), Plaça del Rei, s/n, tel: 93-315 11 11. Tues–Sat 10am–2pm and 4pm–8pm; Sun and holidays, 10am–2pm.

Museu d'Història de Catalunya, Palau de Mar, Port Vell, tel: 93-216 05 00. Tues–Sat 10am–7pm, Wed till 8pm, Sun 10am–2.30pm.

Museu Frederic Marès, Plaça de Sant Iu, 5, tel: 93-310 58 00. Tues–Sat 10am–7pm; Sun and holidays, 10am–3pm.

Museu Marítim, Av. Drassanes s/n, tel: 93-301 18 71. Tues–Sat 10am–7pm.

Museu Nacional d'Art de Catalunya, Palau Nacional, Parc de Montjuïc, tel: 93-423 71 99. Tues–Sat 10am–7pm, Sun 10am–2.30pm.

Museu Picasso, Montcada 15–23, tel: 93-319 63 10. Tues–Sat 10am–8pm, Sun 10am–3pm.

Museu Tèxtil i de la Indumentària, Montcada 12, tel: 93-310 45 16. Tues–Sat 10am–6pm, Sun 10am–3pm.

Palau de la Música, Sant Francesc de Paula 2, tel: 93-268 10 00 or 93-315 11 11. Guided visits only 10.30am–3.30pm but auditorium usually off limits on performance days.

Palau Güell, Nou de la Rambla 3, tel: 93-317 39 74. Guided visits only. Mon–Fri 10am–6.30pm in summer, 10am–5pm in winter.

Parc Güell, Olot s/n,Gràcia, tel: 93-284 64 46. Park, daily 10am–8pm. Casa-Museu Gaudí, summer daily 10am–8pm, winter 10am–6pm. Park is free, charge for museum.

Parc Zoològic (Barcelona Zoo). Daily 9:30am–7:30pm in summer, 10am–5pm in winter.

Poble Espanyol, Marqués de Comillas, tel: 93-325 78 66. Mon, 9am–8pm; Tues–Thur, 9am–2am; Fri–Sat, 9am–4am, Sun, 9am–12am.

Sagrada Família, Carrer de Majorca 401, tel: 93-455 02 47. Summer daily 9am–8pm; winter daily 9am–6pm.

Santa Maria del Mar, Plaça de Santa Maria, tel: 93-310 23 90. Daily 9.30am–1.30pm and 4. 30pm–8pm. Free.

WHAT TO DO

SHOPPING

Barcelona is at least Madrid's equal as a shopping capital. As a city of eminent style and taste, Barcelona abounds in fashion boutiques, antiques shop, and art galleries. Design is taken very seriously here.

Shopping is also extremely pleasant, as the city hasn't yet been overtaken by homogenous American or Euro stores, although there are some shiny new shopping malls. Catalonia still thrives on family-owned shops, and window shopping along the Rambla de Catalunya or Passeig de Gràcia is a delight. Remember that with the exception of the big department stores, most shops are closed between 1.30 or 2pm and 4–5pm, and stay open until 8pm or later. Many smaller stores also close on Saturday afternoon and Sunday.

The best items to look for include fashionable clothing, shoes and leather products; antiques; books (Barcelona is the publishing capital of Spain); high-tech design, home furnishings and objets d'art; and music.

In the Eixample, **Passeig de Gràcia** and **Rambla de Catalunya** are great window-shopping streets, with some of Barcelona's finest fashion, jewellery, and home design shops. The nearby streets Mallorca, Valencia, and Provença are also overflowing with interesting shops. **Avda Diagonal,** which cuts across Barcelona, has some of the finest and most expensive stores in Barcelona. It's where to go if your tastes and your wallet run to Armani.

The area near Las Ramblas is also excellent spots for shopping. Art galleries and young, alternative fashion shops have sprung up in the narrow streets of the Gothic Quarter. **Plaça de Catalunya,** the entrance to the old city, is the

La Boqueria sells every kind of fresh food imaginable, all arranged in tempting displays.

jumping-off point for some of its principal shopping streets. **Portal de l'Àngel** and **Carrer Portaferrisa** are always swarming with shoppers. **La Rambla** itself relies on a heavy tourist trade in trinkets, such as bullfight posters plastered with your name, leather (or plastic) wineskins called *botas*, and their glass relative, the *porrón*; imitation Toledo steel; imitation duelling pistols; and tawdry sex-shop toys. Still, you don't have to look too hard to find succulent pastry shops and creative jewellery stores.

The major department store is **El Corte Inglés**, Spain's biggest. It seems to stock everything for all potential customers and occasions, although it can get crowded. There is the huge, original branch and a new, smaller one on Plaça de Catalunya, one in Portal de l'Àngel specialising in sports and leisure goods, books and music, and one in Avda Diagonal near the Princesa Sofía Hotel. All their branches are open from 10am–10pm. Also in Plaça de Catalunya is a large complex called **El Triangle**, which includes a branch of **Habitat**, and a representative of the French chain, **FNAC** which has the city's best selection of national and foreign music. **La I'lla**, on Avda Diagonal, is one of Barcelona's best upscale shopping malls. In the port area, the **Maremàgnum** mall is teeming with shops and stays open until 11pm. The latest shopping complex to open is a huge one in the newly developed Diagonal Mar by the sea.

Some of the best spots for **antiques** are in the Ciutat Vella. Troll for finds along Banys Nous, de la Palla, and Petritxol, home to innumerable antiques dealers. In the Eixample, **Bulevar dels Antiquaris,** a storefront at Passeig de Gràcia 57, conceals a maze of 70-odd antiques dealers, and there are several individual antiques shops on Mallorca and Valencia.

For **art** purchases, areas worth exploring are Consell de Cent, in the Eixample; Passeig del Born, which has become a hot new gallery area (try Galeria Principal Sombrerers, which specialises in prints and lithographs by new, young artists); and the streets around the contemporary art museum, MACBA, in El Raval, where other galleries are quickly springing up. There are also galleries on Petritxol, near Plaça del Pi, and Montcada, clustered around the Picasso Museum, where you'll also find a number of galleries specialising in reproductions. Ceramics, ranging from traditional tiles, plates, and bowls with blue-and-yellow decoration, to more modern creations, can be found in the streets around the cathedral and along Montcada. A huge selection of good-quality ceramics and handicrafts is sold at **Art Escudellers** (Escudellers 23–25). **BCN Original**, next to the Tourist Information Office at Plaça de Catalunya 17, has a nice selection of good quality souvenirs and gifts.

Spain's publishing industry is headquartered in Barcelona, so it's not hard to find a wide assortment of literature, including many titles in English and other foreign languages. Excellent art books, books on Spanish culture, cookery books, and lots of discounted titles – many in English – are found at **Happy Books,** which has branches on Passeig de Gràcia and Ronda de la Universitat. **Llibrería Francesa,** on Passeig de Gràcia at Provença, has many books in French and English, particularly travel titles. The **Crisol** chain, with a branch on Rambla Catalunya 81, is also very well stocked, as is the huge French store, FNAC, on Plaça de Catalunya. There is an excellent bookshop in the CCCB (Contemporary Culture Centre) in El Raval.

For quintessential Catalan design, **Vinçon** (Passeig de Gràcia 96), Barcelona's premiere design emporium, contains just about everything that could be considered functional and well designed. It stocks expensive lighting and funky furniture, as well as watches, kitchen utensils, and stationery. Vinçon is known for its whimsical display windows. **BD Ediciones de Diseño** (Mallorca 291–3)**,** in a gorgeous *modernista* mansion designed by Domènech i Montaner, deals in classy Catalan design, especially furniture. **Pilma** (Avda Diagonal 403) has some good stock, but with less innate style. Another place to have a look is the small design-oriented shop in the **Museu de Tèxtil i d'Indumentària** (Montcada 12) – expensive but good quality.

Fashion is a serious subject in Barcelona. Look for cool fashions for men and women by **Toni Miró** at his signature store (**Antonio Miró**) at Consell de Cent 349, and at **Groc** on Rambla de Catalunya 100, and Muntaner 385. The Galician designer **Adolfo Domínguez** has shops across Spain; his fashions are slightly more mainstream. In Barcelona, there are branches at Passeig de Gràcia 32 and 89 and Diagonal 570.

Loewe in Casa Lleó Morera, Passeig de Gràcia 35) is Spain's premier upscale leather goods store. Also good for leather (slightly less expensive than Loewe) is Yanko, on Passeig de Gràcia 95. Also on Passeig de Gràcia, **Gonzalo Comella** sells the designs of several labels, including Miró, Armani, and Ermenegildo Zegna.

Going downmarket a bit, **Bulevard Rosa** (Diagonal 474 and 609 and Passeig de Gràcia 55) has a number of excellent shops, including Polo (a Spanish shop, not affiliated with Ralph Lauren). For young and trendy clothes, you can't go wrong with **Zara,** a Spanish chain that has spread successfully all over Europe. There are many branches, the biggest on Passeig de Gràcia at the junction with the Gran Via de les Corts Catalanes. **Mango** also all several outlets in the city.

For foodstuffs, **Colmado Quílez** (Rambla de Catalunya 63), is a classic Catalan emporium, with packaged goods, fine wines, cheeses, and imported beer in a photogenic corner

Some of the shop fronts are as inviting as the goods inside.

shop. For roasted nuts, dried fruits, coffee and spices, go to the 150-year-old **Casa Gispert** (Sombrerers 23) near Santa Maria del Mar. **Escribà** at La Rambla 83, is a beautiful, century-old shop selling wonderful chocolates.

For a religious experience and a history lesson with your foodstuffs shopping, visit **Caelum** (de la Palla 8), which stocks all kinds of products produced by monasteries around the world (beers made by Trappist monks, honey, candles, cheese, etc). Downstairs is a cellar/tea room where ancient foundations of 14th-century baths were uncovered and are now on public view.

The ultimate food shopping experience in Barcelona, of course, is **Mercat La Boqueria** *(see page 26)* for fish, meat, fruit, vegetables, charcuterie and olives. It's open Monday–Saturday till 8pm and its not to be missed.

Barcelona's preeminent flea market is **Els Encants**, which pulsates with action every Monday, Wednesday, Friday and Saturday at Plaça de les Glóries Catalanes (Glóries Metro). Some of it's good, some of it's rubbish, but it's good fun. For stamps and coins, go to the **Plaça Reial** on Sunday morning, or to the **Sant Antoni** market, which also sells records and books. The **Plaça Sant Josep Oriol** has a weekend art fair with artists selling watercolours and oil paintings.

Non-EU residents can reclaim IVA (Value Added Tax, anything from 6 to 33 percent depending on the type of goods); if purchases are substantial (you must spend at least 90 euros in a single store), it is certainly worthwhile filling out the forms in the shop. The refund can be credited to your credit card at the airport or mailed to your home address after your return. You must show your purchases to the customs inspector upon departure and give him the appropriate forms (which you get from stores advertising "Tax Refund").

ENTERTAINMENT

Spaniards have earned a reputation as consummate party goers, and while Barcelona may not be quite as fanatical about late nights as Madrid, it is still a place that really swings when the sun goes down. It has virtually every kind of nightlife, from cool cabarets to live jazz, rock, flamenco, and world music to opera, symphony concerts and theatre, and a thriving bar and disco scene. At night, some streets, like the Rambla and Passeig de Gràcia, become slow-moving rivers of people just walking and talk-

In Barcelona's clubs and dance bars, the action doesn't start till midnight.

ing. The main churches and monuments are illuminated, and the city takes on a new and graceful aspect.

The weekly cultural guide *Guía del Ocio* contains up-to-date information on all entertainment in Barcelona (available at newsstands, in Spanish), while *Barcelona Olé!,* a monthly guide put out by Barcelona Tourism, has information on big shows and performances.

A concert at the **Palau de la Música** (Sant Francesc de Paula 2; tel: 93-268 10 00), the *modernista* masterpiece, is a wonderful experience. It almost doesn't matter what the performance is, but you might see anything from a chamber or symphony concert to contemporary music.

Barcelona's famous opera house, **Gran Teatre del Liceu** (La Rambla, 51–59; tel: 93-485 99 13 or 902-33 22 11;

Barcelona still has many traditional old bars.

<www.liceubarcelona.com>), was gutted by fire in January 1994, but reopened to general acclaim in winter 1999. Tickets are hard to get, despite its increasing seating capacity, but worth a try. The new **Auditori Municipal** (Plaça de les Arts)**,** home of the Barcelona Symphony Orchestra, has a 2,500-seat main auditorium and a smaller one for chamber concerts (for tickets, tel: 902-10 12 12 or <www.obc.es>).

The Caixa Forum, Av. Marquès de Comillas 6 (tel: 902-22 30 40 for information) is a sophisticated new cultural centre that hosts musical performances as well as exhibitions and other events.

For theatre, there is the new **Teatre Nacional**, Plaça de les Arts, tel: 93-246 00 41, with a wide and varied programme; **Lliure**, Montseny 47, tel: 93-218 92 51 for good contemporary productions; and **Mercat de les Flors**, Lleida 59, tel: 93-318 85 99, in a converted flower market stages experimental theatre and contemporary dance. Naturally, most productions are in Spanish or Catalan.

Flamenco is not a Catalan tradition, but some *tablaos* – live flamenco performances – are put on for tourists: **Tablao Flamenco Cordobés** (Las Ramblas 35, tel: 93-317 66 53) is the most popular and predictable, while **El Patio Andaluz** (Aribau 242, tel: 93-209 33 78) also puts on *sevillanas,* traditional Andalusian music. There are also flamenco shows twice nightly, except Monday, at **El Tablao de Carmen** in the Poble Espanyol on Montjuïc (Arcos 9, tel: 93-325 68 95). And there's real flamenco at **Los Tarantos** in Plaça Reial.

Live jazz most nights can be found at **Harlem Jazz Club** in the Gothic Quarter (Comtessa de Sobradiel 8), probably the city's best jazz club. **Jamboree**, in the Plaça Reial, is also good. There are salsa venues, too: try **Sabor Cubano** at Francisco Giner 32, or **Samba Brasil**, Lepant 297.

Two of Barcelona's oldest cabarets, **El Molino** and **Bodega Bohemia**, have recently had to close, although the former was such an institution that campaigners are trying to reopen it. Tastes have changed: **Luz de Gas** (Muntaner 246) used to be a music hall but now presents jazz, rock and soul, and becomes a dance venue after midnight. **Sala Apolo**, another ex-music hall, specialises in rock, pop and reggae.

For nostalgia, there's **Boadas** (Tallers 37), just off the Rambla, the oldest cocktail bar in town, with authentic 1930s decor; and **Pastis**, Santa Monica 4, serving pastis and playing Piaf.

Nick Havanna in Rosselló 208 was the first of the 1980s "design bars". It's still going strong, though not as fashionable as it was. The hottest bar scene at present is in **El Born**, near Santa Maria del Mar. Bars come and go very fast, but currently **Gimlet**, Carrer Rec 24 (a very hip cocktail joint), the **Plastic Bar** (for those who can take their tequila) and **Woman Caballero** (which doesn't even open till 2am) are the favourites.

There are also numerous music festivals: the Festival de Música Antigua is held in April and May (tel: 902-22 30 40), and the Festival de Guitarra de Barcelona takes place in June (tel: 902-10 01 12). One of the best events in the city is **Grec,** an annual festival of international dance, music, and theatre. From the last week of June to the end of the first week in August the cultural calendar is filled with everything from American blues to Brazilian samba and avant-garde European dance. Events are held all over the city, but the most impressive are at the Grec Theatre on Montjuic (for information, tel: 93-301 77 75; <www .grecbcn.com>).

If you're lucky enough to be in the city during a **festival** – either a religious or secular holiday – you'll see the different neighbourhoods erupt into life. Food, fireworks, music, costumes, and especially the huge papier-mâché effigies called *gegants* (giants) and their comical companions, the *cap grossos* (bigheads), are essential fiesta features. Each neighbourhood has its own identifying models. The *gegants* are about 4 metres (13 ft) high and elaborately dressed as kings and queens, knights, ladies, gentlemen, and country people. *Cap grossos,* meanwhile, are usually oversized cartoon heads of well-known personalities. Often they are accompanied by *dracs* (dragons) and *dimonis* (devils).

A constant of Catalan festivals are the *castellers*, acrobatic troupes of men and boys who climb on each other's shoulders to form human towers up to nine men high, the highest level formed by a small boy. This takes place most spectacularly at the festival of La Mercè in honour of the city's patron saint, on 24 September, in the Plaça de Sant Jaume.

The pre-Lent Carnaval is another good excuse to dress up and hold processions and parties. Like most festivals it is accompanied by late-night bands and plenty of fireworks.

The panel on page 94 lists the major events.

SPORTS

Spectator Sports

The 1992 Olympics cemented Barcelona's reputation as a sports-mad city. Barceloneses are wild about Barça, their championship football (soccer) club, and are avid fans of cycling, golf, and auto and motorcycle racing. But they're also active sports enthusiasts, eager to escape the city for a round of golf, sailing, or skiing (only a couple hours away in the Pyrenees). Recreational cycling on Montjuïc and Tibidabo is very popular, and of course swimming and sunbathing – whether at the city beaches or along the Costa Daurada and Costa Brava – is a prime activity.

The great spectator sport in Barcelona is football, and a match involving Barça, one of Europe's perennial champions, can bring the city to a standstill. The club's Camp Nou stadium, in the Barrio Alto, northwest of Diagonal, is the largest in Europe with a seating capacity of 98, 250. Consult a newspaper for dates and times of games. Camp Nou has an excellent football museum, one of the most visited museums in Spain.

Bullfighting is not a Catalan passion, but Barcelona does have a bull ring and *corridas de toros*, even if they don't grab the imagination of locals like they do in Madrid and the south of Spain. You can attend a bullfight at the Plaza de Toros

Cycling is a popular activity in Barcelona.

Monumental (Gran Vía at Passeig de Carles I), on Sunday afternoon at 5pm throughout the summer.

Participant sports

Visitors looking to take active part in the city can join joggers in the parks of Montjuïc or Tibidabo, rent skates or bikes in the Port Olímpic, or play golf at one of the fine courses near the city. Alternatively, visit the **Can Caralleu** sports centre on Tibidabo (tel: 93-204 69 05 for the hours when it is open to non-members), which has tennis, pelota and volley ball courts, and two swimming pools.

Cycling is popular and tourist offices can provide you with a map showing recommended routes and bike lanes and advice about taking bikes on public transport. On Tibidabo, the **Carretera de las Aiguas,** a dirt path that winds along the mountain, with spectacular views of the city below, is a great place to walk, jog, or cycle. **Barcelona by Bicycle** offers easygoing, enjoyable tours around La Ribera, the Gothic Quarter, and the waterfront – one even includes dinner (tel. 93-268 21 05 for more information). They also hire bikes. Bikes can be rented from **Icària Sports**, Av. Icària 180, tel: 93-221 17 78; from **Fillicletos**, Passeig de Picasso 40, tel: 93-319 78 85, where there is easy access to the Parc de la Ciutadella and the waterfront. They have tandems and child seats available.

At the **Reial Club de Golf El Prat**, El Prat de Llobregat, tel: 93-379 02 78 near the airport, 27 holes provide three different circuits. Clubs and carts may be rented, and there's a pool for non-participants. Other nearby courses are at **Sant Cugat**, Sant Cugat del Vallès, tel: 93-674 39 08, off the A-7 motorway just west of the city, which also hires clubs and trolleys and has a pool; and the Terramar course at Sitges, tel: 93-894 05 80. For more information, visit www.catgolf.com.

For sailing information, you can contact the Reial Club Marítim, tel. 93-315 00 07. For water sports and equipment hire in general, try **Base Nautica de la Mar Bella**, Platja de Bogatell, Av. Litoral, tel: 93-221 04 32.

Skiing in the Pyrenees is popular; most resorts are within two hours of Barcelona, some are accessible by train, and there are cheap weekend excursions available. Information can be obtained from the Asociació Catalana d'Estacions d'Esquí, tel: 93-416 09 09, or www.lamolina.com.

BARCELONA FOR CHILDREN

Barcelona is an excellent city for children. Besides the city beaches, the Port Vell waterfront has **L'Aquàrium**, one of the largest aquariums in Europe (Moll d'Espanya, tel. 93-221 74 74) and a 3-D **Imax movie theatre** (tel: 902-33 22 11)l. **The Zoo** (Ciutadella Park, tel: 93-221 25 06), has the world's only albino gorilla in captivity and the park itself, with boats for hire, is fun. **Poble Espanyol** (Montjuïc), a re-creation of a Spanish village, is very popular with families, both locals and visitors. The Tibidabo amusement park (**Parc d'Atraccions** tel: 93 211 79 42) is entertaining, and kids love to arrive there via the Tramvia Bleu *(see page 73)*. In terms of museums, the **Museu de Cera** (Wax Museum), Passatge de la Banca 7, tel: 93-317 26 49, is usually a hit.

Tibidabo for fairground rides with a view.

Calendar of Events

5–6 January *Reis Mags* (Three Kings Day), gift giving and pyrotechnic displays.

February (second week), Feast of Santa Eulàlia, parades of *gegants,* medieval dances.

Feb–March Carnival at the beginning of Lent is a wild celebration. Sitges carnival is the best in the region.

Semana Santa/Easter Holy Week preceding Easter starts with Palm Sunday procession through Rambla de Catalunya. Special religious processions and services on Holy Thursday and Good Friday.

23 April Feast of Sant Jordi (St George), book and flower stalls are set up around the city (La Rambla, Passeig de Gràcia).

27 April Feast of Virgin of Montserrat, liturgical rituals, choir singing, and *sardana* dancing.

11 May Feast of Sant Ponç, herb fair in Carrer de l'Hospital.

mid-June Corpus Christi, carpets of flowers and processions in Sitges. Barcelona has the curious tradition of the "dancing egg" balanced on the spray of the cathedral fountain.

23–24 June Feast of Sant Joan (St John), the major event in Catalonia, with fireworks and feasting.

late June–early August *Grec* festival of theatre, classical, pop, and rock music.

15–21 August Festa Major de Gràcia, parties, parades and fireworks in the festooned streets of Gràcia neighbourhood.

11 September *Diada,* Catalan national day, demonstrations and flag waving.

24 September A week of celebrations, Barcelona's main festival, in honour of the city's patron, Mare del Déu de la Mercè (Our Lady of Mercy). The Rambla becomes an outdoor banquet hall, the squares bandstands, and the streets become dance floors. Particular fun are the Ball de Gegants, a parade of huge papiermachê figures, and Correfoc, a rowdy nocturnal parade of devils and dragons and firecrackers .

6–24 December Santa Llùcia Fair selling Nativity figurines, art, crafts and Christmas trees in front of the cathedral.

EATING OUT

Catalans adore eating, and especially love dining out, the epitome of social activity. They enjoy one of the finest, most imaginative cuisines in Spain, and Barcelona is the best place to sample its rich variety. The cooking is well prepared but not stuffy: an attractive mix of haute cuisine and the traditional rustic cooking that's fed Catalanes for centuries.

Barcelona's restaurants begin with a major advantage: superb ingredients, as anyone who's entered a great covered market in the city can attest. Catalan cooking is based on *cucina del mercat* – market cuisine. Since Barcelona is a Mediterranean port, fresh fish and shellfish lead the menus (even though they're often flown in from the north coast and Galicia). Fruits and vegetables, exported to the rest of Europe, are at their freshest. Mountain-cured hams and spicy sausages, spit-roasted meats, and fowl with aromatic herbs are specialities. Expect *all i oli* (a kind of garlic and olive oil mayonnaise), produce from the countryside, and wild mushrooms – *setas* – an object of obsession for people all over Catalonia.

Barcelona's cosmopolitan population enjoys food of every Spanish region; Basque cookery is especially appreciated (Basque *tapas* bars have sprouted like the wild mushrooms Catalanes love so much). International cuisine used to mean just French, but the roster of restaurants from all over the world has grown by leaps and bounds in the past decade. Most recommended restaurants are in the Old Quarter and the Eixample, though the hottest dining area is along the waterfront, in the new port and increasingly in El Born. The most exclusive restaurants tend to be in the Barrios Altos residential neighbourhoods north of the Eixample. Eating out in Barcelona is a treat and can be one of the highlights of your trip. Restaurants are not cheap, but they compare favourably

with the cost of eating out in many European and North American capitals. Sometimes menus are offered only in Catalan, so you should always ask if there is one in English or Spanish.

Meal times

For many visitors, eating hours in Spain take some getting used to. Barceloneses, like all Spaniards, eat late by most standards. Lunch is served between 1 and 4pm, but usually isn't eaten until 2.30 or 3pm.

Carnivore's delight: hams and sausages on a stall in La Boqueria market.

Dinner is served from about 8pm until 11.30 pm, though on weekends people sometimes don't sit down to dinner until after midnight. Visitors aren't required to dine as late as locals, and you can usually get a meal at almost any time of the day, but if you enter a restaurant soon after the doors have swung open, you are likely to find yourself dining alone or with other foreign visitors. However, you could always adopt the Spanish system, which is to pace yourself for the late hours by eating *tapas*.

Restaurants and Menus

When eating out, Spaniards generally eat a three-course meal at both lunch and dinner, including dessert and coffee. However, it's not uncommon to share a first course, or unheard of to order *un sólo plato* – just a main course – if you're not that hungry or looking to economise. Many restaurants offer a lunchtime *menú del día* or *menú de la casa*, a daily set menu that is a really good bargain. For a fixed price you'll get three courses: a starter, often soup or salad, a main dish, and dessert (ice-cream, a piece of fruit or the ubiquitous flan, a kind of caramel custard), plus wine, beer or bottled water, and bread. Typically, the cost is about half of what you'd expect to pay if you ordered from the regular menu. Most Spaniards will also order the *menú,* so there's no need to think you're getting the "tourist special".

You can also eat cheaply in *cafeterías*, where you will usually be offered a *plat combinat* (*plato combinado* in Spanish), usually meat or fish with chips and salad, served on the same plate. Not the best way to eat, but fast and inexpensive.

Reservations are recommended at Barcelona's more popular restaurants. Prices generally include service, but it's customary to leave a 5–10 percent tip.

Restaurants feature a grading system, from five forks to one, marked on the door; signs are supposed to announce the category, as well, though they are not always prominently displayed. The system indicates price and grades the elaborateness of the facilities and service, not the quality of the food.

Your choices are not limited to restaurants and cafeterias. Most cafés and bars (also called *tabernas*, *bodegas,* and *cervecerías*) serve food, often of a surprisingly high standard. Here you can have a selection of *tapas*, sandwiches (*bocadillos* in Spanish, *bocats* or *entrepans* in Catalan), or limited *plats combinats*.

Breakfast is a trivial affair in most of Spain, Barcelona included, except at hotels, which offer mega-buffets as money-makers or enticements. (Check to see if breakfast is included in the room price at your hotel; if not, the hefty price may prompt you to try the nearest café or cafeteria.) Locals usually have a *café con leche* accompanied by bread or toast or a pastry, such as a croissant. The occasional bar and cafeteria may serve not only great coffee but an "English breakfast" of bacon and eggs, too.

Tasty Tapas

Tapas – the often not-so-small snacks for which Spanish bars and cafés are world-famous – come in dozens of delicious varieties, from appetisers such as olives and salted almonds to vegetable salads, fried squid, garlicky shrimp, lobster mayonnaise, meatballs, spiced potatoes, wedges of omelette, sliced sausage and cheese. The list is virtually endless, and can be surprisingly creative, especially at the now very popular Basque tapas joints. A dish larger than a *tapa* is called a *porción*. A large serving, meant to be shared, is a *ración*, and half of this, a *media ración*. Best of all, *tapas* are usually available throughout the day.

> *Tapa* means "lid", a name derived from the little plate used to cover the beverage glass – and to carry the snack – back in the days when a drink always came with a free morsel of food.

Local specialities

The foundation of rustic Catalan cuisine is *pa amb tomàquet* – slices of rustic bread are rubbed with garlic and halves of beautiful fresh tomatoes, doused with olive oil, and sprinkled with salt. Another typical Catalan dish is *espinacs a la catalana,* spinach prepared with pine nuts, raisins and garlic. Others include *escudella* (Catalan stew); *suquet de peix* (fish and shellfish soup); *botifarra* (white Catalan sausage, often with white beans) and *fuet* (long, dry sausage); and *fideus* (long, thin noodles served with pork, sausage and red pepper). A popular local fish served in a variety of ways is *rape* (angler fish), especially tasty prepared *a l'all cremat* (with burnt garlic). Other good bets are *mero al forn* (baked sea bass) and *llenguado a la planxa* (grilled sole). You might be fooled by the Catalan word for a Spanish *tortilla* (omelette), which is *truita*, but translates as both omelette and trout. *Bacallà*, the lowly salt cod, is now served in the most distinguished restaurants in various guises. A *sarsuela* is a stew of fish cooked in its own juices; a *graellada de peix* is a mixed grill of fish.

Other specialities are *llebre estofada amb xocolata* (stewed hare in a bitter-sweet chocolate sauce). Barcelona's all-purpose sausage is the hearty *botifarra*, often served with *faves a la catalana* (young broad beans stewed with bacon, onion and garlic in an earthenware casserole). *Xató* (pronounced sha-toe) is the endive-and-olives salad of Sitges, fortified with tuna or cod, and has an especially good sauce made of red pepper, anchovies, garlic, and ground almonds. The word for salad of any kind is *amanida*.

Although it originates in rice-growing Valencia, the classic seafood *paella* is probably high on every visitor's list of dishes to sample in Barcelona. Try the restaurants in Barccloneta for a paella of fresh mussels, clams, shrimp, and several kinds of fish. It will take about 20 minutes to prepare.

When it comes to dessert, *flan* is ubiquitous, but there's a home-made version, the more liquid *crema catalana* (egg custard with caramelised sugar on top). *Mel i mato* is a treat made with honey and creamy cheese. The greatest sweets are those delightful delicacies sold in pastry shops.

Drinks

Wine is a constant at the Catalan table. In addition to a wide assortment of fine wines from across Spain, including Rioja, Navarra, and Ribera del Duero, Barcelona presents an opportunity to try some excellent regional wines. Those from Penedès, the grape-growing region just outside Barcelona where *cava*, Spain's sparkling wine, is produced, are excellent. *Cava* itself goes perfectly with seafood and *tapas*. Among Penedès reds, try Torres Gran Coronas, Raimat, and Jean León. Wines from the Priorato area are superb, robust, expensive reds that rival the best in Spain. Don't be surprised to be offered red wine chilled in hot weather.

Spanish beers, available in bottles and on draft, are generally light and refreshing. A glass of draught beer is a *caña*. *Sangría* is a favourite summer wine and fruit punch – many bars have their own recipe, but it's drunk more by visitors than locals.

You'll find every kind of sherry (*jerez*) here. The pale, dry *fino* is sometimes drunk not only as an apéritif but also with soup and fish courses. Rich dark *oloroso* goes well after dinner. Spanish brandy varies from excellent to rough: you usually get what you pay for. Other spirits are made under licence in Spain, and are usually pretty cheap. Imported Scotch whisky is fashionable, but expensive.

Coffee is served black (*solo*), with a spot of milk (*cortado/tallat*), or half and half with hot milk (*con leche*). There

is the usual array of international soft drinks available, and sometimes freshly-squeezed orange juice. A popular non-alcoholic drink is *horchata de chufa*, made with. *Horchaterías* are street bars that specialise in *horchata* and ice cream.

The long-established Café Zurich has had a recent facelift.

To Help You Order…

Could we have a table?	**¿Nos puede dar una mesa, por favor?**
Do you have a set menu?	**¿Tiene un menú del día?**
I'd like a/an/some…	**Quisiera…**
The check, please	**La cuenta, por favor (El compte, por favor)**

…and Read the Menu

cerveza	**beer**	leche	**milk**
pan	**bread**	langosta	**lobster**
calamares	**squid**	bocadillo	**sandwich**
postre	**dessert**	arroz	**rice**
pescado	**fish**	ensalada	**salad**
azúcar	**sugar**	helado	**ice cream**
agua (fresca)	**(iced) water**	vino	**wine**
verduras	**vegetables**	atún	**tuna**
mariscos	**shellfish**	bacalao	**codfish**
mejillones	**mussels**	cocido	**stew**
boquerones	**fresh anchovies**	morcilla	**blood sausage**
callos	**tripe**	cangrejo	**crab**
caracoles	**snails**	pollo	**chicken**
cerdo	**pork**	pulpitos	**baby octopus**
champiñones	**mushrooms**	queso	**cheese**
puerco	**pork**	jamón serrano	**cured ham**
ternera	**veal**	gambas	**prawns**
cordero	**lamb**	res	**beef**
tortilla/truita	**omelette**	entremeses	**hors-d'oeuvre**
chorizo	**pork sausage**	flan	**carmel custard**
judías	**beans**	asado	**roasted**
poco hecho	**rare**	al punto	**medium**
muy hecho	**well done**	a la parilla/	**grilled**
al ajillo	**in garlic**	a la plancha	

HANDY TRAVEL TIPS

An A–Z Summary of Practical Information

A Accommodation 103
Airport 103
B Bicycle Rental 104
Budgeting for your
Trip 104
C Car Hire 105
Climate 106
Clothing 106
Crime and Safety 106
Customs and Entry
Requirements 107
D Driving 107
E Electricity 110
Embassies and
Consulates 110
Emergencies 111
G Gays, Lesbians 111
Getting There 111
Guides and Tours 113
H Health and Medical
Care 114

Holidays 115
I Internet 115
L Language 116
M Maps 117
Media 117
Money 118
O Opening Hours 119
P Police 120
Post Offices 120
Public
Transport 121
R Religion 123
T Telephone 123
Time Zones 124
Tipping 124
Toilets 125
Tourist Information
Offices 125
W Web Sites 126
Weights and
Measures 127
Women's Issues 127
Y Youth Hostels 127

A

ACCOMMODATION (*hotel; alojamiento*) (See also the list of
RECOMMENDED HOTELS starting on page 128)
The Olympic Games set off a much-needed hotel building boom in
Barcelona, but accommodation can often be hard to come by. Advance
reservations are strongly recommended. Spanish hotels are rated by a
star system, with five star deluxe the top grade. The classifications often seem arbitrary, with some two- and three-star places fully as good
as others rated higher. About two-thirds of the city's hotels fall into the
three- and four-star categories. Breakfast is rarely included in the room
rate, and hotels are subject to a 7 percent IVA (value added tax).

For economy budgets, there are several hundred star-rated guest
houses (*hostales, pensiones*) and youth hostels (*albergues de juventud*).

I'd like a double/single room.	**Quisiera una habitación doble/sencilla.**
with/without bath/shower	**con/sin baño/ducha**
double bed	**cama matrimonial**
What's the rate per night?	**¿Cuál es el precio por noche?**
Is breakfast included in the room rate?	**¿Está incluído el desayuno?**
Where's an inexpensive hotel?	**¿Dónde hay un hotel económico?**

AIRPORT (*aeroport; aeropuerto*)
Barcelona's international airport, El Prat de Llobregat (tel: 93-928 38 38)
is 12 km (7 miles) south of the city. The distribution of flights in the three
terminals may vary so confirm from which your flight will depart. There
are tourist information and hotel reservation booths in Terminal A.

You can get into Barcelona by train, bus or taxi). The national train
service, **Renfe** (tel: 902-24 02 02), runs trains from just outside the air-
port. They leave every half hour, stopping at Estació de Sants and Plaça
Catalunya, taking about 20 minutes. The fare is 2.60 euros. The
Aerobús departs every 15 minutes from all three terminals for Plaça de
Catalunya, stopping at numerous points en route. The fare is 3.50 euros

single, 5.65 return. **Taxis,** lined up outside the terminals, charge about 12–18 euros to the centre of the city. Make sure you have agreed a fare before you start.

B

BICYCLE RENTAL (*Alquiler de bicicletas*)

Bicycles can be rented at several outlets, such as Fillicletos, Pg de Picasso 40, tel: 93-319 78 85 and Icària Sport, Av. Icària 180, tel: 93-221 17 78; Barcelona-by-Bike tel: 93-268 21 05 also offers tours.

BUDGETING FOR YOUR TRIP

Barcelona is on the whole, with a favourable exchange rate, cheaper than other major European cities, such as London, Paris, or Rome.

Transport to Barcelona. For Europeans, Barcelona is a short, direct flight away. As well as regularly scheduled flights there is a good choice of discounts and charter flights, especially those booked on the Internet, e.g. Easy Jet at http://easyjet.com and Go, at www.go-fly.com. For those travelling from beyond Europe, the flight will be a considerably greater proportion of your overall budget, though you may also be able to find packages and specials. You are much less likely to have to fly through Madrid than was once the case.

Accommodation. Hotels in Barcelona, along with Madrid, are the most expensive in Spain, but many at the three- and four-star level are comparatively good value. Keep in mind that most do not include breakfast or the 7 percent IVA (value added tax). See approximate prices in the "Recommended Hotels" section, starting on page 128. It is always wise to book ahead.

Meals. Restaurant prices are not cheap, though with a favourable exchange rates, even top-rated restaurants may be surprisingly affordable compared to many European capitals. The *menú del día,* a prix-fixe midday (and sometimes evening) meal, is an excellent bargain. Spanish wines are an excellent deal, even in fine restaurants.

Local transport. Public transport within the city – buses and the metro –is inexpensive *(see page 121)* and taxis are an affordable way to get around.

Incidentals. Your major expenses will be excursions, entertainment, and daytime sporting activities. Nightclub and disco cover prices are high, as are drink prices once inside.

C

CAR HIRE *(coches de alquiler)*
Unless you plan to travel a good deal throughout Catalonia, there is no need to rent a car (the excursions included on pages 74–78 are all easily accessible by public transportation). A car in Barcelona, a city with considerable parking problems and general congestion, would cause more trouble that it's worth.

If you wish to rent a car, however, major international companies – Avis, Hertz, Budget, National – and Spanish companies have offices in the airport and in the city centre. A value-added tax (IVA) of 15 percent is added to the total charge, but will have been included if you have pre-paid before arrival (normally the way to obtain the lowest rates). Fully-comprehensive insurance is required and should be included in the price; confirm that this is the case. Most companies require you to pay by credit card, or use your card as a deposit/guarantee.

You must be over 21 and have had a licence for at least 6 months. A national driver's licence will suffice for EU nationals; others need an international licence.

I'd like to rent a car (tomorrow).	**Quisiera alquilar un coche (para mañana).**
for one day/a week	**por un día/una semana**
Please include full insurance.	**Haga el favor de incluir el seguro a todo riesgo.**
Unleaded gasoline	**petrol sin plomo**
Fill it up.	**Lleno, por favor.**

Barcelona

CLIMATE

Barcelona's mild Mediterranean climate assures sunshine most of the year and makes freezing temperatures rare even in the depths of winter, December to February. Spring and autumn are the most agreeable seasons. Mid-summer can be hot and especially humid; at times a thick smog hangs over the city.

		J	F	M	A	M	J	J	A	S	O	N	D
max.	°F	55	57	60	65	71	78	82	82	77	69	62	56
	°C	13	14	16	18	21	25	28	28	25	21	16	13
min.	°F	43	45	48	52	57	65	69	69	66	58	51	46
	°C	6	7	9	11	14	18	21	21	19	15	11	8

CLOTHING (*ropa*)

Barceloneses are very stylish and fashion-conscious. Smart casual clothing is what visitors generally need. Men are expected to wear a jacket in better restaurants and nightclubs. Jeans and sports shirts are fine in informal bars and restaurants, but you won't see many local people eating out in shorts and trainers, except in beach-side cafés. From November to April you'll need a warm jacket or sweater and raincoat. The rest of the year, light summer clothing is in order.

Do I need a jacket? A tie?	¿Se necesita una americana?
	¿Una corbata?

CRIME AND SAFETY

You should exercise caution and be on your guard against pickpockets and bag snatchers (especially be wary of people offering "assistance"), as in any large city, especially on or near the Rambla, the old city (particularly El Raval) and other major tourist areas, such as La Sagrada Família and crowded spots such as markets. Be careful about deserted alleyways, especially at night. Don't leave luggage unattended; don't carry more money than you'll need for daily expenses; use the hotel safe for larger sums and valuables; photocopy personal documents and leave the originals in your hotel; wear cameras strapped crosswise on your body; don't leave video cameras, car stereos, and valuables in view inside a car, even when locked. The blue-clad mobile anti-crime squads are out in force on the Ramblas and principal thoroughfares. Should you be the victim of any crime, make a *denuncia* at the nearest police station (*comisaría*) (vital if you are going to make an insurance claim). The City Police, headquartered at Ramblas 43, tel: 93-301 90 60, has a special tourist assistance scheme. There is usually someone on duty who can speak English. and there are interpreter services available at Via Laietana 49, tel: 93-302 63 25.

I want to report a theft.	**Quiero denunciar un robo.**
My handbag/ticket/wallet/ passport has been stolen	**Me han robado el bolso/el billete/la cartera/el pasaporte.**
Help! Thief!	**¡Socorro! ¡Ladrón!**

CUSTOMS AND ENTRY REQUIREMENTS *(aduana)* (See also EMBASSIES AND CONSULATES on page 110)
For members of EU countries the process is easy: you won't even get your passport stamped (although you still need to carry it). Visas are needed by non-EU nationals unless their country has a reciprocal agreement with Spain. Full information on passport and visa regulations is available from the Spanish Embassy in your country.

As Spain is part of the EU, free exchange of non-duty-free items for personal use is permitted between Spain and other EU countries. However, duty-free items are still subject to restrictions. There are no limits on the amount of money, Spanish or foreign, that you may import
Currency restrictions: Visitors may bring up to 6,000 euros into or out of the country without a declaration. If you intend to bring in and take out again larger sums, declare this on arrival and departure.

I have nothing to declare.	**No tengo nada a declarar.**

D

DRIVING
In the event of any problem drivers have to produce a passport, a valid driver's licence, registration papers, and Green Card interna-

tional insurance which comes complete with a Bail Bond, obtainable from your own insurance company.

Road Conditions. Roads within Barcelona are very congestedand the ring roads around the city can be confusing. Roads and highways outside Barcelona, along the coast and through the interior of Catalonia and to the Pyrenees, are excellent, though you'll have to pay a toll (*peaje/peatje*) on most *autopistas* (motorways). When crossing the La Jonquera border with France (160 km/100 miles) from Barcelona, take the A7 motorway.

Rules and Regulations. Your car should display a nationality sticker. Front and rear seat belts are compulsory. Most fines for traffic offences are payable on the spot. Driving rules are the same as throughout Europe: Drive on the right, overtake on the left, yield right of way to vehicles coming from the right (unless your road is marked as having priority). Speed limits are 120 km/h (75 mph) on motorways, 100 km/h (62 mph) on dual carriageways, 90 km/h (56mph) on other main roads, 50 km/h (30 mph), or as marked, in urban areas. Spaniards appear to disregard speed limits, but that doesn't mean you should.

The roads are patrolled by the Traffic Civil Guard (*Guardia Civil de Tráfico*) on motorcycles. Courteous and helpful, they are also tough on lawbreakers. Don't drink and drive. The permitted blood-alcohol level is low and penalties stiff.

Fuel Costs. Service stations are plentiful throughout Barcelona and Catalonia. *Petrol* (gasoline) comes in 95 (Euro super lead-free), and 98 (lead-free super plus) grades, but not all can be found at every petrol station. Diesel fuel is widely available.

Parking. Finding a place to park can be extremely difficult in Barcelona. Look for "blue zones" (denoted by a blue "P"), which are metered areas, or underground parking garages (also marked with a big blue-and-white "P") and considered the safest bet.

Breakdowns and Assistance. For emergencies, dial **112**. On motorways there are SOS boxes. Also useful is the RACC (Royal Automobile Club of Catalonia), tel: 900-36 55 05. Garages are efficient, but repairs may take time. Spare parts are readily available for Spanish-built cars and other popular models. For other models, they may have to be imported.

Road signs. Most signs are the standard pictographs used throughout Europe. However, you may encounter the following written signs in Spanish, often amended in Catalan.

¡Alto!	Stop!
Aparcamiento	Parking
Autopista	Motorway
Ceda el paso	Give way (yield)
Cruce peligroso	Dangerous crossroads
Curva peligrosa	Dangerous bend
Despacio	Slow
Peligro	Danger
Prohibido adelantar	No overtaking (passing)
Prohibido aparcar	No parking

Car registration papers	**Permiso de circulación**
Are we on the right road for...?	**¿Es ésta la carretera hacia...?**
Full tank, please.	**Lléne el depósito, por favor.**
normal/super/unleaded	**normal/super/sin plomo**
Please check the oil/tires/battery.	**Por favor, controle el aceite los neumáticos/la batería.**
Can I park here?	**¿Se puede aparcar aquí?**
My car has broken down.	**Mi coche se ha estropeado.**
There's been an accident.	**Ha habido un accidente.**

Barcelona

(International) Driving Licence **Carnet de conducir (internacional)**

Car-registration papers **Permiso de circulación**

Green card **Tarjeta verde**

Fluid measures

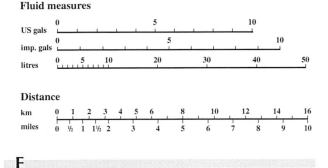

Distance

E

ELECTRICITY *(corriente eléctrica)*

The standard is 220 volts, but some hotels have a voltage of 110–120 in bathrooms as a safety precaution. Check before plugging in any appliance.

Sockets (outlets) take round, two-pin plugs, so you will probably need an international adapter plug. Visitors from North America will need a transformer unless they have dual-voltage travel appliances.

What's the voltage? **¿Cuál es el voltaje?**

an adapter/a battery **un transformador/una pila/ una batería**

EMBASSIES AND CONSULATES *(embajadas; consulados)*

Almost all Western European countries have consulates in Barcelona. All the embassies are in Madrid.

Australia Gran Vía Carles II, 98, 9°, tel: 93-490 90 30

Canada Passeig de Gràcia 17°; tel: 93-204 27 00

Ireland Gran Vía Carles III, 94, tel: 93-491 50 21

UK Avinguda Diagonal 477, 13º, tel. 93-366 62 00

US Passeig de la Reina Elisenda,23, tel: 93-280 22 27

Where's the British/American consulate?	**¿Dónde está el consulado británico/americano?**

EMERGENCIES (See also EMBASSIES AND CONSULATES, HEALTH AND MEDICAL CARE, POLICE, and CRIME AND SAFETY) The National Police emergency number (in and outside Barcelona) is **091**; dial **092** for municipal police and **080** in the event of fire.

Careful!	**Cuidado**	Police!	**Policia**
Fire!	**Fuego**	Stop!	**Deténagase**
Help!	**Socorro**	Stop thief!	**ladrón**

G

GAY AND LESBIAN TRAVELLERS (*homosexual; gay*; *lesbiana*) Barcelona has an active gay community and scores of clubs and nightlife options. Conservative Catholic beliefs still predominate, though, in many sectors, so gay visitors may wish to be discreet. The gay and lesbian hotline is tel: 900 601 601. The free magazine *Nois* has information and listings of clubs, restaurants, and other entertainment options. Casal Lambda, Ample 15, te:l 93-319 55 50 is a gay cultural centre (open from 5pm).

GETTING THERE

Air Travel (See also AIRPORTS)
Barcelona's airport is linked by regularly scheduled daily non-stop flights from across Europe. Some flights from the US and Canada are direct; others still go through Madrid (or in some cases, Lisbon). From Australia and New Zealand, regular one-stop flights go directly to Barcelona or Madrid. Flying times: London, about two hours; New York, approximately eight hours. Iberia, the Spanish national airline, covers most countries in shared arrangements with their own carriers.

Barcelona

There are frequent scheduled flights between Barcelona and Madrid and other Spanish cities on Iberia (tel: 902 400 500), Air Europa (tel: 902 401 501), and Spanair (tel: 902 131 415).

International Airport. Barcelona's international airport is El Prat de Llobregat (tel: 93-298 38 38), 12 km (7 miles) south of the city centre.

By Sea.
Ferries and cruise ships enter Barcelona's Estació Marítim. **Buquebus** is the fastest Mallorca ferry (3 hours). Departures from Barcelona are daily at 8am; Friday and Saturday at 8am and 4pm. Return trips from Palma leave Friday and Sunday at 8pm and midnight, other days at 7:30pm. Contact Buquebus (tel: 902 414 242; fax: 93-412 35 90; www .buquebus.com) for further information and bookings. **Transmediterránea** (tel: 902 454 645; www.trasmediterranea.es) also operates ferries to the Balearic islands; most of the year they take about eight hours but in summer, there's an express ferry that takes about four hours.

Rail travel.
Passengers generally have to change trains at the Spanish frontier, as the Spanish tracks are of a wider gauge than the French. Exceptions are the luxury high-speed Talgo and the Trans-Europ-Express, which have adjustable axles.

Trains are one of the best ways to get around Spain, and are efficient and modern. The Talgo arrives at Estació de França (near Parc de la Ciutadella; metro: Arc de Triomf). the rest go to Estació Sants (metro: Sants). RENFE is the Spanish national train network; tel: 902 240 202 for national services, 902 243 402 for international trains. Local trains in Catalonia are serviced by the provincial government, Ferrocarrils Generalitat de Catalunya (FGC) (tel: 93-205 15 15).

RENFE honours Inter-Rail, Rail-Europ, and Eurail cards (the latter sold only outside Europe), and offers substantial discounts to young people under 26 and senior citizens (over 65). It is well worthwhile finding out about current discount tickets from a travel agency, local railway station, or, in Barcelona, from the information desk in Sants station or by phoning RENFE on the number above.

By car.
The highways outside of Barcelona are generally excellent, and cars travel very fast. The A-7 motorway leads to Barcelona from France and northern Catalonia, the A-2 leads to Barcelona from Madrid, Zaragoza, and Bilbao. From Valencia or the Costa del Sol, take the E-15 north.

GUIDES AND TOURS *(guías; visitas guiadas)*
English-speaking, licensed guides and interpreters may be arranged through the **Barcelona Guide Bureau** (tel: 93-268 24 22; email: bgb@bcn.servicom.es) or City Guides, tel: 93-412 06 74. Hotels and travel agencies will also advise on guides and interpreters.

Tours by bus: **Barcelona Bus Turístic** offers a tour of 24 city sights with two different routes; get on and off as you please. Both depart from Plaça de Catalunya at 9am daily; all stops have full time-tables. Complete journey time is about 3 hours. The bus runs year-round except for 25 December to 1 January. Tickets may be purchased on board or in advance at Turisme de Barcelona, Plaça de Catalunya, tel: 906 301 282.

By foot: **Barcelona Walking Tours** has English-speaking, guided tours of the Gothic quarter every Saturday at 10am. Walks (90 minutes) begin at Turisme de Barcelona, Plaça de Catalunya, tel: 906 301 282.

By bicycle: **Barcelona by Bicycle** (Espartería 3, tel: 93-268 21 05) leads easygoing bike tours around the Old City and the waterfront (one tour includes dinner).

Architecture tours: The **Ruta del Modernisme** (Modernist Route) allows visitors to take in numerous important *modernista* buildings. You get a ticket and a map offering a 50 percent discount at each site that permits visits (some, such as the Palau de la Música and Palau Güell, are guided visits, most are independent). Tickets and information from Passeig de Gràcia 41, tel: 93-488 01 39. The **Gaudí Tour** lasts four hours and takes in the major sites. Tickets and information: Centre Cultural Caixa Catalunya, tel: 93-484 89 09.

We'd like an English-speaking guide.	**Queremos un guía que hable inglés.**
I need an English interpreter.	**Necesito un intérprete de inglés.**

H

HEALTH AND MEDICAL CARE

Standards of hygiene are high, and medical care in Barcelona is generally excellent. Most doctors speak sufficient English to deal with foreign patients. The water is safe to drink, but bottled water is always safest (and tastes better); it is inexpensive and available everywhere. *Agua con gas* is carbonated, *sin gas* is still water.

Visitors from EU countries with corresponding health insurance facilities are entitled to medical and hospital treatment under the Spanish social security system – you need form E111. However, it doesn't cover everything and it is advisable to take out private medical insurance, which should be part of a travel insurance package.

For emergencies, go to the "Urgencias" department of a main hospital: **Hospital Clinic**, Carrer de Casanova 143, tel: 93-227 54 00; **Hospital Cruz Roja**, Carrer Dos de Maig 301, tel: 93 433 15 51; go to an **ambulatorio** (medical centre) or tel: **061** for an ambulance.

Pharmacies *(farmacias)* operate as a first line of defence, as pharmacists can prescribe drugs and are usually adept at making on-the-spot diagnoses. Pharmacies open during normal business hours but there is always one in each district that remains open all night and on holidays. The location and phone number of this *farmacia de guardia* is posted on the door of all the others.

Where's the nearest (all-night) pharmacy?	**¿Donde está la farmacia (de guardia) más cercana?**
I need a doctor/dentist.	**Necesito un médico/dentista.**

HOLIDAYS *(fiestas)*

1 January	*Año Nuevo*	New Year's Day
6 January	*Epifanía/Reis Mags*	Epiphany
1 May	*Festa del Treball*	Labour Day
23–24 June	*Sant Joan*	St John's Day
15 August	*Assumpció*	Assumption
11 September	*Diada*	Catalan National Day
24 September	*La Mercè*	Barcelona's patron saint
1 November	*Tots Sants*	All Saints' Day
6 December	*Día de la Constitució*	Constitution Day
8 December	*Immaculada Concepció*	Immaculate Conception
25–26 December	*Navidad*	Christmas

Movable dates:

Jueves Santo: late March/April	Holy Thursday
Viernes Santo: late March/April	Good Friday
Lunes de Pascua: late March/April	Easter Monday
Corpus Christi: mid-June	Corpus Christi

INTERNET

There are several sites in Barcelona where internet access is cheap and easy. Try: **easyInternet Café** at La Rambla 31 and Ronda Universitat 35, both branches open 24 hours a day; **Net Movil Consulting**, La Rambla 40, is open 10am–10pm daily; **Café Internet**, Gran Via de les Corts Catalanes 656, open Monday–Saturday 9am–midnight; and **Internet Gallery Café**, Barra de Ferro 3, near the Picasso Museum.

Barcelona

LANGUAGE (*idioma; lenguaje*)

Both Catalan (*català*) and Castilian Spanish (*castellano*) are official languages in Catalonia; everyone in Barcelona who speaks Catalan can speak Spanish, but because many residents come from other parts of the country they do not all speak Catalan. Catalan has experienced a huge renaissance, which has much to do with the people's cultural identity, and many of them will not speak Spanish unless it is absolutely necessary. Street signs are in Catalan, but museum labels and menus are usually in both languages.

Learning and using some phrases in Catalan will be appreciated, but Spanish will certainly get you by. Here are a few useful terms:

English	Catalan	Castilian
Good morning	**Bon dia**	*Buenos días*
Good afternoon	**Bona tarda**	*Buenas tardes*
Good night	**Bona nit**	*Buenas noches*
Thank you	**Gràcies**	*Gracias*
You're welcome	**De res**	*De nada*
Please	**Si us plau**	*Por favor*
Goodbye	**Adéu**	*Adiós*
Welcome	**Benvinguts**	*Bienvenido*
See you later	**Fins despr'es**	*Hasta luego*
Hello	**Hola**	*Hola*
Do you speak English?	**¿Parla anglés?**	*¿Habla inglés?*
I don't understand.	**No ho entenç.**	*No entiendo.*
How much is it?	**¿Quant es?**	*¿Cuánto vale/es?*

The *Berlitz Spanish Phrase Book and Dictionary* covers most situations you are likely to encounter during your stay in Barcelona, and includes a menu-reader supplement.

M

MAPS (*planos*)
Since 1985, all street names in Barcelona and most Catalan towns have been posted in Catalan. Several towns have reverted to their Catalan names, too. Lérida is Lleida, San Carlos is Sant Carles, etc. Many maps published earlier than 1985 still have names in Spanish and even quite different names. Some words that may crop up frequently are:

English	Catalan	Castilian
Avenue	**Avinguda**	*Avenida*
Street	**Carrer**	*Calle*
Church	**Església**	*Iglesia*
Palace	**Palau**	*Palacio*
Boulevard	**Passeig**	*Paseo*
Passage/alley way	**Passatge**	*Pasaje*
Square	**Plaça**	*Plaza*

Many Barcelona streets are one-way and/or do not permit turns to the left or right. A good, detailed street map will be of immense assistance. The Guía Urbana de Barcelona handbook is most comprehensive and contains much useful information.

I'd like a street plan.   **Quisiera un plano de la ciudad.**

a road map of this region   **un mapa de carreteras de esta región**

MEDIA (*periódico* = newspaper, *revista*= magazine)
Most European newspapers and the Paris-based *International Herald Tribune* are sold on the day of publication on newsstands in the Ramblas and Passeig de Gràcia and in FNAC in Plaça de Catalunya. Principal European and American magazines are also widely available. *Metropolitan*, Barcelona's first monthly magazine in English is free and has useful listings. For Spanish-speakers the *Guía del Ocio* (Leisure Guide) lists bars, restaurants, cinema, theatre, and concert performances.

Barcelona

Most hotels and bars have television, usually tuned to sports (international or local), and broadcasting in Castilian and Catalan. Satellite dishes are sprouting, and most tourist hotels offer multiple channels (German, French, Sky, BBC, CNN, etc.). Reception of Britain's BBC World Service radio is usually good.

Have you any English-language newspapers/magazines?	**¿Tienen periódicos/revistas en inglés?**
Where's a newspaper kiosk?	**¿Dónde hay un kiosco?**

MONEY (*dinero; efectivo*)

Currency (*moneda*). Since January 2002 the monetary unit of Spain has been the euro. Notes are issued in denominations of 5, 10, 20, 50, 100, 200 and 500 euros. Coins in circulation are 1, 2, 5, 10, 20, 50, centimos and 1 and 2 euros. Pesetas can be exchanged indefinitely in any branch of the Banco de España.

Currency exchange. Banks and *caixes* (savings banks) are the best place to exchange currency, offering the best rates with no commission. Many travel agencies and *casas de cambio* (displaying a *cambio* sign) will also exchange foreign currency and stay open outside banking hours (see page 119). Be wary of those advertising "no commission" – their rates are much lower, so you are in effect paying a hefty commission. Banks and exchange offices pay slightly more for traveller's cheques than for cash. Always take your passport when you go to change money.

Credit cards (*tarjetas de crédito*). Most major international cards are widely recognised, though smaller businesses tend to prefer cash. Credit cards linked to Visa/Eurocard/MasterCard are most generally accepted. They are also useful for obtaining cash advances from banks. A credit card will usually give you the highest exchange rate, translated at the time of billing rather than the moment of transaction.

ATMs. Cash machines are now ubiquitous in Spain and you'll find them all over Barcelona.

Traveller's Cheques. *(cheques de viajero)*. Throughout Barcelona, hotels, shops, restaurants, and travel agencies all cash traveller's cheques, and so do banks, where travellers are practically guaranteed to get a better rate – you will always need your passport. Try to cash small amounts at a time, keeping some of your cheques stowed away in the hotel safe; and keep the individual numbers of your cheques separately so they can be replaced quickly if they are lost or stolen.

Where's the nearest bank/currency exchange office?	**¿Dónde está el banco/la casa de cambio más cercana?**
I want to change some pounds/dollars.	**Quiero cambiar libras/dólares.**
Do you accept traveller's cheques?	**¿Acceptan cheques de viajero?**
Can I pay with a credit card?	**¿Se puede pagar con tarjeta?**
How much is that?	**¿Cuánto es/Cuánto vale?**

O

OPENING HOURS

The big department stores remain open all day, but most shops close in the middle of the day. Usual hours are from 9am–2pm and 4–8pm Monday–Saturday, although these hours do vary.

Post offices are usually open Monday–Friday 9am–2pm, Saturday 9am–1pm (also see Post Offices, page 120). **Banks** generally open Monday–Friday 8.30am–2pm, and Saturday 9am–1pm in winter. **Government offices** and the vast majority of **businesses** are open 9am–2pm and from 4–8pm. In summer, many businesses work *horas* *intensivas*, which means they open from 8am–3pm only, to avoid the hottest part of the day.

Most museums open 9am–1pm and 4–8pm and the majority close on Monday.

P

POLICE *(policía)*

Spanish municipal and national police are efficient, strict, and courteous – and generally very responsive to issues involving foreign tourists. In Barcelona, dial **092** for municipal police and **091** for national police. The main police station is located at Vía Laietana 43, tel: 93-301 66 66.

Where's the nearest police station?	**¿Dónde está la comisaría más cercana?**

POST OFFICES *(correos/correus)*

Post Offices – all identified by yellow-and-white signs with a crown and the words "Correos y Telégrafos" – are for mail and telegrams; you can't usually telephone from them. The postal system has greatly improved in recent years and is now pretty reliable. Opening hours are usually 9am–2pm Monday–Friday, 9am–1pm Saturday. The Central Post Office, in Plaça Antoni López, at the port end of Via Laietana is open Monday–Friday 9am–9pm, Saturday 9am–1pm..

Stamps *(sellos)* can be purchased at the post office or at *estancs* (tobacconists – look for the brown-and-yellow sign that reads "Tabacs" or "Tabacos"). Rates are divided into four areas of the world, just like telephone calls: the EU, rest of Europe, the US and Canada, and the rest of the world. Allow about one week for delivery to North America, and 4–5 days to the UK. To speed things up, send a letter *urgente* (express) or *certificado* (registered).

Where is the Post Office?	**¿Dónde está el Correo?**

A stamp for this letter/ postcard, please.	**Por favor, un sello para esta carta/tarjeta postal.**
I'd like to send this letter.	**Me gustaría enviar esta carta.**
airmail	**vía aérea**
express (special delivery)	**urgente**
registered	**certificado**
How long will it take to arrive?	**¿Cuánto tarda en llegar?**

PUBLIC TRANSPORT *(transporte público)*

Barcelona has a reliable and comprehensive public transport system; getting around town is easy, rapid and inexpensive. Get an up-to-date bus and train (FEVE) timetable from a tourist information office or any metro station. **Tel: 010** for information on all public transport.

By Bus *(autobús)*. About 70 bus lines crisscross Barcelona. Lines and hours are clearly marked but if it is your first time in the city, the bus may not be the best option. You'll have trouble recognising where you are, and most bus drivers speak no English. With the metro, at least you can clearly identify your stop. But buses are a good way of getting to see more of the city. They run daily 5am–10pm; there are infrequent night buses from 10:30pm–5am. You can buy a ticket from the driver, or purchase a multiple card *(tarjeta multi-viaje T-10)* which is punched inside the bus. This is valid for bus, metro and urban FGC lines; it can be bought at metro stations, banks or *estancs* and is very good value.

By Metro The Metro is excellent, modern and clean. Its five lines are by far the fastest and easiest way to navigate the city. The city has begun to implement tri-lingual directions and audio (in Spanish, Catalan, and English). Stations are marked by a red diamond symbol. Single-ticket fares and 10-trip tickets *(see above)* are available, the latter a nearly half-price bargain. The metro runs Monday–Thursday 5am–11pm, Friday and Saturday 5am–2am;

Barcelona

holidays 6am–11pm and Sunday 6am–midnight. Good pocket-sized maps are available at metro stations.

Regional FGC (Ferrocarrils Generalitat de Catalunya) trains also travel to Barcelona's upper neighbourhoods Gràcia, Sarrià, Pedralbes, and Tibidabo and to nearby towns such as Terrassa and Sabadell. Unless you are going to one of these destinations, make sure the train you board (most likely at Plaça de Catalunya) is a metro and not an FGC train – it's easy to confuse them.

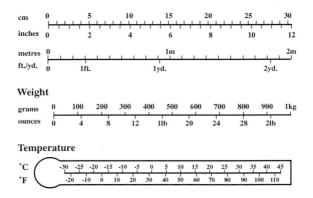

By Taxi. Black-and-yellow taxis are everywhere and affordable. During the day, they aren't your best option, as traffic is very heavy in the city. At night, especially if you've dined in the old quarter, taxis are the best way to return to your hotel or continue on with the night (have the restaurant call if you don't feel comfortable waiting for one on the street). Hail a cab in the street or pick one up where they're lined up (usually outside hotels). A green light and/or a *libre* (vacant) sign shows when the cab is empty. Reputable taxi companies include **Radio Móvil** (tel: 93-

358 11 11), **Radiotaxi Verd** (tel: 93-266 39 39) and **Taxigroc** (tel: 93-490 22 22). Check the fare before you get in; rates are fixed and are displayed in several languages on the window. Also ensure that the meter has been reset when you begin your journey. Refuse a cab if the driver claims the meter is not working.

When's the next bus/train to…?	**¿Cuándo sale el próximo autobús/tren para…?**
bus station	**estación de autobuses**
A ticket to…	**Un billete para…**
single (one-way)	**ida**
return (round-trip)	**ida y vuelta**
What's the fare to…?	**¿Cuánto es la tarifa a …?**

R

RELIGION (*religión; servicios religiosos*)
Roman Catholicism is the religion of Catalonia (and all Spain) and Mass is said regularly in the churches of Barcelona, great and small. There are churches of most major faiths; the tourist information office at Plaça de Catalunya has information on religious services, including those in foreign languages. Major ones are: Anglican: St George's Church, Sant Joan de la Salle 41, tel: 93-417 88 67 (Sunday, 11am); Judaism: The Synagogue Avenir 24, tel: 93-200 61 48; Islam: Centro Islàmico, Av. Meridiana 326, tel: 93- 351 49 01.

T

TELEPHONE (*teléfono*).
Spain's country code is **34**. Barcelona's local area code, **93**, must be dialled before all phone numbers, even for local calls.

The telephone office is independent of the post office and is identified by a blue-and-white sign. You can make direct-dial local, national and international calls from public phone booths (*cabinas*) in the street. Most operate with coins and cards; international phone credit cards can also be used. Instructions for use are given in several languages in the booths. For most calls at pay phones, it's easier to use a phone card (*tarjeta telefónica*), which can be purchased at any post office or *estanc* (look for the sign "Tabacos" or "Tabacs"). To make an international call, dial 00 for an international line + the country code + phone number, omitting any initial zero. Calls are cheaper after 10pm on weekdays, after 2pm on Saturday, and all day Sunday. For national telephone information, dial **003**. For international information, dial **005**.

You can also make calls at public telephone offices called *locutorios*. These are much quieter than making a call on the street. A clerk will place the call for you and you pay for it afterwards.

Local, national, and international calls can also be made from hotels, but almost always with an exorbitant surcharge. Make them with an international calling card, if you must make them from your hotel room. (Before departure, be sure to get the international access code in Spain for your long distance telephone carrier at home.)

You can send a fax from the main post office or from most hotels, though the charge can be high in the latter. At **Prisma-fax**, Jaume I 18, fax: 93-319 58 65, you can send and receive faxes.

| Can you get me this number in…? | **¿Puede comunicarme con este número en…?** |

TIME ZONES

Spanish time is the same as that in most of Western Europe – Greenwich Mean Time plus one hour. Daylight Saving Time is in effect from the last Sunday in March to the last Sunday in September; clocks go forward one hour in spring and back one hour in autumn, so Spain is generally one hour ahead of London, the same as Paris, and six hours ahead of New York.

| What time is it? | **¿Qué hora es?** |

TIPPING *(propina; servicio)*
Since a service charge is normally included on hotel and restaurant bills, tipping is not obligatory but it's usual to leave a small coin (about 5 percent of the bill) on a bar counter, and 5–10 percent on restaurant bills. If you tip taxi drivers, 5 percent is enough unless they are especially helpful. Additional guidelines:

Hotel porter, per bag	60 centimos.
Lavatory attendant	25 centimos
Tour guide	10 percent
Hairdresser	10 percent
Taxi Driver	5 percent
Maid, for extra services	60 centimos–1 Euro

Is service (tip) included?	**¿Está incluído el servicio?**

TOILETS
There are many expressions for "toilets" in Spanish: *aseos, lavabos, servicios,* and *W.C.* The first two are the most common. Toilet doors are distinguished by a "C" for "*Caballeros*" (gentlemen) or "S" for "*Señoras*" (ladies) or by a variety of pictographs.

In addition to the well-marked public toilets in main squares and stations, a number of neat coin-operated toilets in portable cabins marked "W.C." are installed around the city. Just about every bar and restaurant has a toilet available for public use. It is considered polite to buy a drink if you drop in to use the conveniences.

Where are the toilets?	**¿Dónde están los servicios?**

TOURIST INFORMATION OFFICES *(oficinas de información turística)*
There are Spanish National Tourist Offices in many countries. These include:

Australia: International House, Suite 44, 104 Bathurst St, P.O. Box A-675, 2000 Sydney NSW, tel: (02) 264 79 66

Barcelona

Canada: 2 Bloor St. West, Suite 3402, Toronto, Ontario M4W 3E2, tel: 416-961 31 31

UK: 22-23 Manchester Square, London W1U 3PX tel: 0207 486 8077; brochure line: tel: 09063 640 630

US: Water Tower Place, Suite 915 East, 845 North Michigan Ave, Chicago, IL 60611, tel: 312-944 0216/642 1992

8383 Wilshire Blvd, Suite 960, 90211 Beverly Hills, CA 90211, tel: 213-658 7188

666 5th Ave, 35th floor, New York, NY 10103, tel: 212-265 88 22

1221 Brickell Ave., Ste. 1850, Miami, FL 33131, tel: 305-358 19 92

Barcelona: For general information, tel: 010. The main office is Turisme de Barcelona, Plaça de Catalunya, tel: 906 301 282; from abroad 93-368 97 30, open daily 9am–9pm. The Tourism Information Office in the Ajuntament, Plaça Sant Jaume, is open Mon–Sat 10am–8pm, Sun and holidays 10am–2pm. Informació Turística de Catalunya, Palau Robert, Passeig de Gràcia 107, tel. 93-238 40 00; www.gencat.es/probert. provides information about the entire region; open Mon–Fri 10am–7pm, Sat 10am–2pm. There are also information offices at Sants station and the airport.

Where is the tourist office?   **¿Dónde está la oficina de turismo?**

 W

WEB SITES

There are a number of websites that will provide you with plenty of useful information about Barcelona before you start your trip. Try: Barcelona Ajuntament (City Hall): www.bcn.es

Catalonia on the web: www.gencat.es

Spain on the web: www.spaintour.com/indexe.html

National Tourist Office: www.tourspain.es

WEIGHTS AND MEASURES

Spain uses the metric system. A conversion chart is shown below. There is also a chart on page 110 showing conversions for longer distances and liquid measurements.

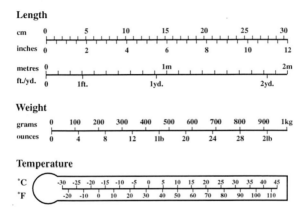

Length

Weight

Temperature

WOMEN TRAVELLERS

Women won't encounter harassment just walking around or eating alone, though – as anywhere – one should obviously avoid quiet streets after dark. A good source of information on women-related issues is: Librería Pròleg, Dagueria, 13. This is the city's specialist bookshop for feminist subjects and women writers. It is also an exhibition space and holds talks occasionally.

Y

YOUTH HOSTELS

Hostal de Joves: Passeig de Pujades 29; tel/fax 93-300 31 04 (near Parc de la Ciutadella).

Kabul, Plaza Reial 17, tel: 930318 51 90, fax: 93-419 301 40 34.

Mare de Déu de Montserrat, Mare de Déu de Coll 41–52, tel: 93-210 51 51, fax: 93-210 07 98.

Pere Tarrès, Numància 149, tel: 93 410 23 09, fax: 93-419 62 68.

Recommended Hotels

Many new hotels, mostly of the four- and five-star category, were built in Barcelona in preparation for the 1992 Olympic Games. At the time it seemed that there would be a glut of rooms available after the games ended, but as the city has continued to increase in popularity, this has definitely not been the case.

Hotels of greatest interest to most visitors are those in the Eixample, the commercial and *modernista* grid north of Plaça de Catalunya, or in the Ciutat Vella, which includes La Rambla and the Barri Gòtic. Along the waterfront there is still only one luxurious high-rise hotel. Many visitors choose to stay on or near La Rambla, though they have to tolerate late-night noise and crowds. Most mid-level to luxury hotels are either along La Rambla or in the Eixample.

Weekend rates and special deals are available at many hotels. Most hotel rates do not include breakfast or IVA, the 7 percent value-added tax. Be sure to ask about these. The following guide indicates prices for a double room in high season (prices should be used as an approximate guide only):

€€€€€	above 150 euros
€€€€	100–150 euros
€€€	70–100 euros
€€	45–70 euros
€	under 45 euros

Eixample

Alexandra Hotel €€€€ *Carrer Mallorca 251; tel: 93-467 71 66; fax: 93-487 21 24.* A business-like hotel between Rambla de Catalunya and Passeig de Gràcia – an excellent location. Rooms are not large, but are comfortable and nicely furnished. Interior rooms are quieter than those facing the street. Wheelchair access. 85 rooms. Major credit cards.

Gran Hotel Havana €€€€ *Gran Vía de les Corts Catalanes 647; tel: 93-412 11 15; fax; 93-412 26 11; web site <www. hoteles-silken.com>.* A hip and high-tech hotel opened in an 1872 mansion on Gran Via in 1991. Deluxe accommodation at a not unreasonable price. Barcelona's signature design elements are in every detail. Wheelchair access. 145 rooms. Major credit cards.

Hotel Astoria €€€€ *París 203; tel: 93-209 83 11; fax::93-/202 30 08; web site <www.derbyhotels.es>.* A sophisticated and quiet hotel in the upper regions of the Eixample, near La Rambla de Catalunya and a few paces from prime shopping territory on Diagonal. Originally built in the 1950s, the Astoria has been redone and is quite elegant, certainly one of the best three-star hotels in Spain. Some rooms have small sitting rooms or garden terraces. Wheelchair access. 117 rooms. Major credit cards.

Hotel Avenida Palace €€€€ *Gran Vía de les Corts Catalanes 605; tel: 93-301 96 00; fax: 93-318 12 34.* The place to stay if Barcelona's high-tech design craze seems too functional and cold. A luxurious, ornate hotel in the heart of La Rambla, on a busy thoroughfare. Rooms are spacious and elegant. Wheelchair access. Popular with upscale tour groups. Wheelchair access. 160 rooms. Major credit cards.

Hotel Claris €€€€€ *Carrer de Pau Claris 150; tel: 93-487 62 62; fax: 93-215 79 70; web site <www.derbyhotels.es>.* One of Barcelona's most elegant hotels, in the heart of the Eixample. Very high-tech design behind the façade of the Vedruna Palace and guests-only museum of Egyptian art. Rooms, many of which are split-level and even two-story, exude cool chic, combining antiques and Catalan design. Small rooftop pool. Wheelchair access. 120 rooms. Major credit cards.

Barcelona

Hotel Comtes de Barcelona €€€€€ *Passeig de Gràcia 73-75; tel: 93-488 22 00; fax: 93-467 47 85; web site <www .condesdebarcelona.com>*. With an ultra-chic address, just a block from Gaudí's La Pedrera, this popular hotel occupies two impressive former palaces on opposite corners of Passeig de Gràcia. Rooms are modern, large, and elegant, decorated in bright colours. A favourite of architects, designers, and European and Japanese tourists. Wheelchair access. 183 rooms. Major credit cards.

Hotel Duques de Bergara €€€€ *Carrer de Bergara 11; tel: 93-301 51 51; fax: 93-317 34 42.* A luxury, four-star hotel just off Plaça de Catalunya, in a handsome 19th-century townhouse expanded to seven floors. The hotel has a relaxed but elegant feel, and service is top-notch, although rooms are quite small. Wheelchair access. 150 rooms. Major credit cards.

Hotel Granvia €€–€€€ *Gran Via Corts Catalanes 642; tel: 93-302 50 46; fax: 93-318 99 97.* A small hotel with Old World style, occupying a 19th-century palace in a choice location, operating since the 1930s. Smallish but clean rooms, outfitted with antiques. Good value. Wheelchair access. 147 rooms. Major credit cards.

Hotel Majestic €€€€ *Passeig de Gràcia 68; tel: 93-488 17 17; fax: 93-488 18 80; web site <www.nexus.es/colon>*. A large, long-time favourite Recently refurbished from the ground up. Two restaurants, including the exclusive Drolma. Wheelchair access. 331 rooms. Major credit cards.

Hotel NH Calderón €€€€ *Rambla de Catalunya 26; tel: 93-301 00 00; fax: 93-412 41 93. web site <www.nh-hoteles. es>*. Part of the NH chain, depended upon by Spanish business travellers for efficient, handsomely decorated hotels with a wide range of amenities and excellent service. The Calderón is right on the Rambla, a superb location. Comfortable rooms. Rooftop pool. Wheelchair access. 253 rooms. Major credit cards.

Hotel Regente €€€€ *Rambla de Catalunya 76 (Eixample); tel: 93-487 59 89; fax: 93-487 32 27; e-mail <rivoli@alba.mssl.es>.* A mid-sized hotel in a handsome 1913 modernista townhouse on La Rambla de Catalunya. Rooms are standard and modern, renovated in 1997. Rooftop pool. Wheelchair access. 79 rooms. Major credit cards.

Hotel Ritz €€€€€ *Gran Vía de les Corts Catalanes 668; tel: 93-318 52 00; fax: 93-318 01 48; web site <www.ritzbcn.com>.* A 1919 Belle Époque hotel, the Ritz is the city's classic place to stay. Ultra-luxurious and white-glove grand, on a splendid tree-lined avenue in the Eixample. Formal guest rooms, some with marble fireplaces. A couple even have Roman-style baths with rich mosaics. Wheelchair access. 127 rooms. Major credit cards.

Ciutat Vella

Hotel Allegro €€€€ *Portal de l'Àngel 17; tel: 93-318 41 41; fax: 93-301 26 31; web site <www.hoteles-catalonia.es>.* This is a new hotel, on one of Barcelona's busiest pedestrian shopping streets near the Barri Gòtic and La Rambla. Rooms are large and well-furnished, and there's a very nice garden patio. A good choice if you want to be in the thick of it. Wheelchair access. 74 rooms. Major credit cards.

Hotel Colón €€€€ *Avinguda de la Catedral 7; tel: 93-301 14 04; fax: 93-317 29 15; web site <www.nexus.es/colon>.* The closest you can get to the heart of the Barri Gòtic– right across the square. Sixth-floor rooms have large terraces; ask for one with a cathedral view. Renovated in 1992, but the décor is dated. Wheelchair access. 147 rooms. Major credit cards.

Gran Hotel Barcino €€€€ *Carrer Jaume I 6; tel: 93-302 20 12; fax: 93-301 42 42.* Just off the Plaça de Sant Jaume, in the heart of the Barri Gòtic, this modern hotel is chic and well designed. The large, airy lobby outclasses the rooms, though. Wheelchair access. 53 rooms. Major credit cards.

Hotel Barcelona €€€€ *Casp 1–13; tel: 93-302 58 58; fax: 93-301 86 74.* A stone's throw from Passeig de Gràcia and Plaça de Catalunya, this is a functional choice for small groups and business travellers. Wheelchair access. 72 rooms. Major credit cards.

Hotel España €€–€€€ *Carrer Sant Pau 11; tel: 93-318 17 58;. fax: 93-317 11 34.* This nostalgic hotel on the lower part of La Rambla, may not be the place it once was, but it retains enough flavour of by-gone days to recommend it as a good value. The beautiful public rooms were decorated by *modernista* architect, Domènech i Montaner. Guest rooms are plain but clean and large. No air conditioning. 90 rooms. Major credit cards.

Hotel Gaudí €€€ *Nou de la Rambla 12; tel: 93-317 90 32; fax: 93-412 26 36; web site <www.hotelgaudi.es>.* An affordable hotel right across from one of Gaudí's earliest works, the Palau Güell, and just off La Rambla. Very convenient; clean, comfortable, simple rooms. Wheelchair access. 73 rooms. Major credit cards.

Hotel Gótico €€€€ *Jaume I 14; tel: 93-315 22 11; fax: 93-315 21 13.* In the heart of the Ciutat Vella, this medium-sized and well-run hotel was entirely renovated in late 1999. Upgraded to four stars, it has swanky touches of Catalan haute design, and is just a block from Plaça Sant Jaume. 81 rooms. Major credit cards.

Hotel Jardí €€ *Plaça Sant Josep Oriol 1; tel: 93-301 59 00; fax: 93-318 36 64. e-mail <sgs11osa@encomix.es>.* A perfectly placed small hotel in the Barri Gòtic, overlooking two of the prettiest plazas in Barcelona. Jardí rooms are a bargain, though a plaza view costs a little more. Recently renovated and very popular so book well ahead. 42 rooms.

Hotel Oriente €€€ *Ramblas 45–47; tel: 93-302 25 58; fax: 93-412 38 19.* Nostalgic, and right on La Rambla, this was Barcelona's first official hotel. Both Ernest Hemingway and Hans Christian Anderson stayed here. Lots of character. Wheelchair access. 150 rooms. Major credit cards.

Hotel Regencia Colón €€€€ *Carrer Sagristans 13–17; tel: 93-318 98 58; fax: 93-317 28 22.* A couple of paces from the cathedral, this is a good, moderately-priced choice. Although slightly old-fashioned, it is quite popular with tourist groups. Wheelchair access. 55 rooms. Major credit cards.

Hotel Rialto €€€ *Carrer de Ferrán 42; tel: 93-318 52 12; fax: 93-318 53 12.* A small and modern hotel located near the cathedral. Wheelchair access. 63 rooms. Major credit cards.

Hotel Rivoli Rambla €€€€€ *La Rambla 128 ; tel: 93-302 66 43; fax: 93-317 50 53. e-mail <rivoli@ alba.mssl.es>.* A busy townhouse hotel right on Las Ramblas, within inches of the never-ending parade just beyond the front door. Smallish rooms. Fitness centre, Jacuzzi, and solarium on the terrace. Frequent deals available. Wheelchair access. 90 rooms. Major credit cards.

Hotel San Agustí €€€ *Plaça Sant Agustí 3; tel: 93-318 1658; fax: 93-317 29 28.* A comfortable, traditional hotel in a central location. Wheelchair access. 77 rooms. Major credit cards.

Hotel Suizo €€€ *Plaça de l'Àngel 12; tel: 93-310 61 08; fax: 93-310 40 81.* Close to the cathedral, this intimate hotel has a turn-of-the-century air and is comfortable and friendly. Wheelchair access. 51 rooms. Major credit cards.

Le Meridien Barcelona €€€€€ *Ramblas 111; tel: 93-318 62 00; fax: 93-301 77 76.* This imposing hotel sits on a corner of Las Ramblas, but inside, guests are removed from the action and noise. Stylish and tasteful, it's long been a top choice of pop stars performing in Barcelona. Wheelchair access. 206 rooms. Major credit cards.

Nouvel Hotel €€€ *Santa Ana 18–20; tel: 93-301 82 74; fax: 93-301 83 70.* On a pedestrian-only street between La Rambla and Portal d'Àngel, in one of the city's busiest but most atmospheric sections, this small hotel has a wonderful *modernista* lobby. Rooms are comparatively plain, but well equipped. Wheelchair access. 72 rooms. Major credit cards.

Waterfront (Vila Olímpica)

Hotel Arts €€€€€ *Passeig de la Marina 19–21; tel: 93-221 10 00; fax: 93-221 10 70; web site <www.ritzcarlton.com>.* A high-tech, ultra-deluxe modern high-rise, one of Barcelona's two sky-scrapers right on the beach in Vila Olímpica. Extremely efficient, decorated with sophisticated, understated taste. Large rooms, huge bathrooms, and amazing views of the Mediterranean and the city. Wheelchair access. 455 rooms. Major credit cards.

DIAGONAL

Hotel Princess Sofía Intercontinental €€€€ *Plaça Pius XII 4; tel: 93-330 71 11; fax: 93-330 76 21.* A high-rise, luxury, four-star hotel in a good location for business travellers, just off the Diagonal, near banks and the central business district. Less convenient for sightseers. Swimming pool. Wheelchair access. 505 rooms. Major credit cards.

Hotel Rey Juan Carlos I €€€€€ *Diagonal 661; tel: 93-448 08 08; fax: 93-448 06 07.* A premier business traveller's choice, this huge five-star hotel in the business zone has every amenity and ser-vice a demanding guest could want. It's far from the old centre of Barcelona, at the west end of the Diagonal. Several restaurants, swimming pool, and full health club. Wheelchair access. 505 rooms. Major credit cards.

Recommended Restaurants

Dining out is a prime social activity in Barcelona. Catalan cooking is one of the finest regional cuisines in Spain, and there are many atmospheric restaurants that serve it in both hearty and haute versions. Barcelona's roster of Catalan and Spanish restaurants and *tapas* bars is now complemented by a wide selection of international and continental (and even fast food) restaurants. The best areas in which to eat are the Ciutat Vella, which includes the Barri Gòtic, La Ribera and El Born, and the area around La Rambla; the Eixample modern district; and the waterfront area near the Port Olímpic, which is where the most explosive recent growth has taken place.

Remember that local people eat lunch and dinner late *(see page 96)*. You can either join them in eating early-evening *tapas*, to stave off the hunger pangs, or go just after restaurants have opened, when foreign visitors are likely to be the only diners. (Many restaurants close between lunch and dinner. Those that do not are noted below.)

It's wise to make advance reservations, especially at the pricier establishments. The price guides below reflect the cost of an à la carte, three-course meal for one, without drinks.

€€€€	above 35 euros
€€€	24–25 euros
€€	12–24 euros
€	under 12 euros

Ciutat Vella
(Barri Gòtic; La Ribera; La Rambla)

Agut €–€€ *Carrer Gignàs, 16; tel: 93-315 17 09.* Open daily for lunch and dinner (closed August). This small, 75-year-old

135

restaurant is hidden away on a small street in the Barri Gòtic. Relaxed and homely, it has plenty of Catalan flavour and lots of daily specials from the Catalan menu, which might include home-made caneloni, fish, or game. The excellent and huge rice dishes are meant to be shared. Major credit cards.

Agut d'Avignon €€€–€€€€ *Carrer de la Trinidad (Avinyó 8); tel: 93-302 60 34.* Open daily for lunch and dinner (closed August). A 40-year-old, rustic restaurant in a small alley in the Barri Gòtic. The Catalan cooking is creative and hearty, the ambience informal, the prices high. Tremendous wine cellar. Major credit cards.

Cal Pep €€–€€€ *Plaça de les Olles, 8; tel: 93-310 79 62.* Open Monday–Saturday, lunch and dinner. A boisterous bar at the edge of La Ribera, near Santa María del Mar, this is the place for some of the finest and freshest seafood in Barcelona—if you can get a seat. No reservations, and just one row of chairs at the counter and a few tables tucked away in the back room. The counter is the place to be. The display of baby squid, octopus, fried fish, mussels, and more is amazing. Major credit cards.

Can Culleretes €–€€ *Carrer Quintana 5; tel: 93-317 30 22.* Open Tuesday–Saturday for lunch and dinner; Sunday lunch only. Barcelona's oldest restaurant has served traditional Catalan food since 1786. It is cozy and informal, and serves food classics like *espinacas a la catalana* (spinach with pine nuts and raisins) and *butifarra* (white sausage). Fixed-price menus are available weekdays both day and night. Major credit cards.

Casa Leopoldo €€€ *Sant Rafael 24; tel: 93-441 30 14.* Tucked away in the Barrio Chino, this restaurant serves excellent fish and is popular with those who know. Major credit cards.

El Gran Café €€–€€€ *Carrer Avinyó 9; tel: 93-318 79 86.* Open Monday–Saturday for lunch and dinner. Looks like an English pub on the outside, but has a handsome *modernista* interior with red velvet stairs and large mirrors. The set menu is very good value, otherwise rather expensive. Major credit cards.

Els Quatre Gats €€ *Carrer de Montsió 3; tel: 93-302 41 40.* Open Monday–Saturday for lunch and dinner. "The Four Cats," the one-time hangout of Picasso and friends, serves simple Catalan fare in fabulous *modernista* surroundings. It has tapas menu and the *menú del día* is a good deal, but really the atmosphere's the thing. Major credit cards.

Hofman €€€€ *Argentería 74; tel: 93-319 58 89.* Seriously good food cooked by cordon bleu chefs in a cosy atmosphere. Booking essential. Expensive but worth it. Major credit cards.

La Pizza Nostra € *Carrer Montcada, 29; tel: 93-319 90 58.* Open Tuesday–Sunday for lunch and dinner. This small and friendly place just down the road from the Picasso Museum has a good selection of pizzas and pastas, some very creative. Major credit cards.

Los Caracoles €€–€€€ *Carrer Escudellers 14; tel: 93-302 31 85.* Open for lunch and dinner daily without interruption. "The Snails" is famous for its chicken roasting on a spit outside, on one of the old quarter's busiest pedestrian streets. To get to the atmospheric dining room, diners pass through the rowdy kitchen. Los Caracoles has been around since 1835, and while it's touristy it is fun, and you can also get a fine meal of fish, game, roasted chicken, or lamb, in addition, of course, to snails. Major credit cards.

Barcelona

Quo Vadis €€€€ *Carme 7; tel: 93-302 40 72.* Open Monday–Saturday for lunch and dinner. A longtime favourite of Barceloneses, especially opera-goers (the Liceu Opera House is only a couple of minutes away). With several small and casually elegant dining rooms, the feeling is intimate and relaxed, the Spanish menu classy. Major credit cards.

Restaurant España €–€€ *Sant Pau 9; tel: 93-318 17 58.* Open for lunch and dinner daily. A good-value restaurant that could easily be on a sightseeing tour; part of the Hotel España, the restaurant was decorated by *modernista* architect Domènech i Montaner, and the back room has murals by Ramón Casas, a contemporary of Picasso. There's a simple and straightforward set-priced menu for both lunch and dinner, making it a good deal. Major credit cards.

Senyor Parellada €€–€€€ *Carrer Argentaría 37; tel: 93-310 50 94.* Open Monday–Saturday lunch and dinner. An attractive and popular restaurant just up from Santa María del Mar in La Ribera. Both the surroundings and the creative Catalan menu are sophisticated but unpretentious. Major credit cards.

Taxidermista €€ *Plaça Reial 8; tel: 93-412 45 36.* The best choice in the plaza, this former taxidermist's premises has minimalist decor and imaginative food. The set lunch menu is particularly good value. Major credit cards.

Waterfront/Port Olímpic

Agua €€€ *Passeig Marítim 30; tel: 93-225 12 72.* Open daily for lunch and dinner. A modern and attractive place right on the beach, Agua (Water) is an anchor of the waterfront restaurant scene. Well prepared and affordably priced fish, rice dishes such as risottos, and vegetarian dishes. More fun at lunch time. Book early for a seat on the terrace. Major credit cards.

Can Ganassa €€ *Plaça de Barceloneta 4; tel: 93-221 67 39.* Open Thursday–Tuesday for lunch and dinner without interruption. A popular seafood restaurant on the main square in Barceloneta with excellent fish dishes and a wide array of tapas and sandwiches. Major credit cards.

Lungomare Ristorante €–€€ *Marina 16–18; tel: 93-221 04 28.* Open Monday–Saturday lunch and dinner; Sunday lunch only (closed September). Overlooking the Olympic port, with views of yachts, this unpretentious place has pizzas and pastas, as well as good, simple fish and meat dishes. Informal and familiar, though with a handful of more exotic dishes. Major credit cards.

Restaurante Set Portes €€€ *Passeig Isabel II 14; tel: 93-319 30 33.* Open daily for lunch and dinner without interruption. One of Barcelona's most venerable institutions, this has been a favourite for business meals and special occasions since 1836. Sete Portes (meaning seven doors) is famous for its rice dishes; favourites include black rice with squid in its own ink and an assortment of paellas. Portions are very large and the dining rooms are elegant. Major credit cards.

Talaia Mar €€€ *Marina 16 (Port Marítim); tel: 93-221 90 90; web site <www.talaia-mar.es>.* Open daily for lunch and dinner. One of the best new examples of Barcelona's fascination with design, this Talaia Mar has a sweeping bay window overlooking the port, the city's newest dining scene. A creative Mediterranean and seafood menu, with a grilled fish of the day. Major credit cards.

Barcelona

Travi Mar €€–€€€ *Maremàgnum, Moll d'Espanya, local 110, 1st floor; tel: 93-225 81 36.* Open for lunch and dinner daily without interruption. A dependable seafood restaurant with a nautical theme and well prepared, if unsurprising, fish and shellfish. The views of the surrounding port are superb. Good entertainment for restless children is available nearby. Major credit cards.

Eixample

Botafumeiro €€€€ *Gran de Gràcia 81; tel: 93-218 42 30.* Open daily for lunch and dinner without interruption. Barcelona's top seafood restaurant is the king of Spain's favourite. It's large and informal, with lots of action. Much of the fresh seafood is flown in daily from the owner's homeland, Galicia. Great shellfish and seafood tapas here (which keep costs down if you're conscientious). To get a seat at the seafood bar, go at off-hours—noon–1pm for lunch, 7–8pm for dinner. Just north of the Diagonal, at the beginning of the Gràcia neighbourhood. Major credit cards.

Casa Calvet €€€–€€€€ *Casp 48; tel: 93-412 40 12; web site <www.gulliver.es/casacalvet.htm>.* Open Monday–Saturday for lunch and dinner. Located on the first floor of one of Antoni Gaudí's first apartment buildings, Casa Calvet exudes elegant *modernista* ambience. The service is extraordinary, and tables are spaced well apart; some even occupy private booth areas. The Catalan menu is excellent and fairly priced. Major credit cards.

Mordisco € *Rossellón 265; tel: 93-415 76 76.* Open daily for breakfast, lunch, and dinner without interruption. Near the Eixample's major *modernista* sights and shopping, a convenient place for a fast lunch. Extensive list of sandwiches and more elaborate dishes. Friendly and efficient. Major credit cards.

Taktika Berri €€–€€€ *Carrer Valencia 169; tel: 93-453 47 59.* Open for lunch and dinner daily without interruption. Basque cooking is the finest regional cuisine in Spain, and Basque restaurants are popping up everywhere. One of the best in Barcelona is this family-owned and -operated tapas bar and restaurant in a converted textile workshop. The *pintxos* (tapas) are excellent, as are their creative entrées. Try the splendid desserts. Major credit cards.

Tragaluz €€€ *Passeig Concepción, 5; tel: 93-487 01 96.* Open daily for lunch and dinner. Barcelona's love affair with food comes to life in this trendy, colourful restaurant on a tiny passageway off Passeig de Gràcia. The main menu is creative, but there's also a selection of low-fat and veggie dishes, as well as a separate sushi restaurant downstairs. Major credit cards.

TAPAS

Bar Pinotxo € *Mercat La Boqueria, La Rambla.* Open daily for breakfast and lunch. This tiny, plain-looking bar with a handful of stools is surrounded by La Boqueria's mesmerising produce. It's a terrific place to stop when your stomach's beginning to growl. The fish, as you would imagine, is incredibly fresh. Full lunch *menú* (recited orally) also available. No credit cards.

Bar Turó € *Tenor Viñas 1, Parc Turó; tel: 93-200 69 53.* Open daily for lunch and dinner, all-day tapas. Tucked away in the upscale residential neighbourhood north of the Diagonal is this tapas joint, famed throughout the city. Good-value midday menu. Major credit cards.

El Xampanyet € *Montcada 22.* Near the Picasso Museum and El Born this tiled bar specialises in *cava* (hence the name) and some of the best tapas in town, especially the anchovies

Euskal Etxea € *Montcada 1–3; tel: 93-310 21 85.* A great Basque tapas bar with a huge choice that has quickly established itself as a firm local favourite

Irati € *Casanyes 17; tel: 93-200 69 53.* Open for lunch and dinner Tuesday to Sunday. This immensely popular Basque tapas joint, just off La Rambla at the edge of the Barri Gòtic, is always packed. At lunchtime and in early evening, heaping trays of tapas (*pintxos* in Basque) are laid out on the bar. Like a party, only you keep track of the number of tapas and the glasses of wine or beer you've had, and the cheerful attendants tally it up. No credit cards.

La Bodeguita € *Rambla de Catalunya 100; tel: 93-215 48 94.* Open for lunch and dinner daily; closed Monday. It's easy to pass by this simple bodega (next to Toni Miró's Groc fashion boutique). Regulars pop in at any hour for *jamon serrano* and a glass of Rioja. Good wine selection. No credit cards.

INDEX

Ajuntament 32–33

Banys Nous, Carrer del 38
B.D. Ediciones de Diseño 52, 54
Barcelona Stock Exchange 64
Barceloneta 23, 59–61
Barri Gòtic 23, 30–40

cable cars 23, 62, 69, 75
Café de l'Opera 27
Call 37–38
Capella de Sant Jordi 32
    de Santa Àgata 35
    de Santa Llúcia 31
Casa Amatller 49
Casa Batlló 50–51
Casa Lleó Morera 48–49
Casa Milà 49, 51, 53, 79
Castell de Montjuïc 69
Catedral 30–31 79
Centre d'Art Santa Mònica 29
    de Cultura Contemporània 64
    Excursionista de Catalunya 36
Codorníu 78
Col.legi d'Arquitectes 40

Diagonal 71, 76
Diagonal Mar 62

El Raval 22, 24, 64–66
Els Quatre Gats 40, 49
Escribà 25
Escudellers, Carrer de 29
Estadi Olímpic 70

Fundació Antoni Tàpies 47, 52,
    55
Fundació Joan Miró 68–69, 79

Gran Teatre del Liceu 26–27
Gràcia (district) 72

Hospital de la Santa Creu 65
Hospital de la Santa Creu i Sant
    Pau 52, 57
Hotel Oriente 27

Illa de la Discordia 48–51

L'Aquárium 60
La Boqueria 26, 28
La Llotja 64
La Moreneta 74–75
La Rambla 23–29, 54, 64
(also see individual Ramblas)
La Ribera 23, 40–45

Maremàgnum 60
Modernisme 23, 25, 38, 48, 49,
    50, 52, 54, 62–63
Moll de Barcelona 60
Moll de Bacreloneta 61
Moll d'Espanya 60
Moll de la Fusta 61
Monestir de Pedralbes 72
Montcada, Carrer de 42
Montjuïc 23, 60, 66–70, 79
Montserrat 74–76
Monument a Colom 29
Museu Arqueològic 68
    Barbier-Mueller 44
    Cau Ferrat 77
    d'Art Contemporani 64, 79
    d'Art Modern 63, 79
    de la Ciència 72
    d'Història de Catalunya 61,
        79

d'Història de la Ciutat 34, 79
de Cera 29
de les Artes Decoratives 71
Etnològic 68
Frederic Marès 36, 79
Maricel 77
Marítim 59–60, 79
Militar 69
Nacional d'Art de Catalunya
    67–68
Picasso 40, 43–44, 80
Romàntic 77
Tèxtil i de la Indumentària
    44, 80

Pabelló Mies van der Rohe 70
Palau d'Esports Sant Jordi 70
    Dalmases 44
    de la Generalitat 32–33
    de la Música Catalana
        45–46, 49
    de la Virreina 25
    del Lloctinent 36
    Güell 27–28, 50, 52, 80
    Nacional 67
    Reial 35
    Reial de Pedralbes 71, 73
Parc de Collserola 73
    Parc de la Ciutadella 63
    Güell 49, 57–59, 80
    Zoológic 63
Passeig de Gràcia 46, 48,
    53–55, 64, 71
    del Born 42
Pedralbes 72
Petritxol, Carrer de 39
Pla de la Boqueria 26
Placeta del Pi 39
Plaça d'Espanya 67
    de Berenguer el Gran 36

de Catalunya 24, 40, 46, 54,
    72, 77
de les Glòries Catalanes 71
de Sant Felip Neri 38
de Sant Jaume 32–34, 37
de Sant Josep Oriol 39
de Sant Just 33
del Pi 39
del Rei 35-36
Reial 28
Platja de Barceloneta 61
Poble Espanyol 70, 80
Port Olímpic 62

Quadrat d'Or 46

Rambla de Canaletes 24
    de Catalunya 46, 55
    de les Flors 25
    del Mar 60
    de Santa Mònica 29
    dels Caputxins 27
    dels Estudis 25

Sagrada Família 49, 56–57, 72
Sagrat Cor 72
Sant Pau del Camp 66
Sant Sadurní d'Anoia 77–78
Santa Maria del Mar 40–41, 43,
    79
Santa Maria del Pi 39
Sants Just i Pastor 33
Sarrià 52, 72
Sitges 74, 76–77

Teatre Principal 29
Tibidabo 23, 72–73
Torre de Collserola 73

Vila Olímpica 62
Vilafranca del Penedès 78